The Pregnancy Loss Guidebook

**COPING WELL WITH
PREGNANCY AND INFANT LOSS**

Monica Sholar Anderson

© 2024 by Monica Sholar Anderson

All rights reserved. No part of this publication may be reproduced in any form, or by any means, electronic or mechanical, including photocopying, recording, or any information browsing, storage, or retrieval system, without permission in writing from the publisher.

Published in the United States by Green Life Publishing.
First Green Life Publishing Edition, 2024
First Printing

ISBN 979-8-218-22193-5

Although this publication is designed to provide accurate information in regard to the subject matter covered, the publisher and the author assume no responsibility for errors, inaccuracies, omissions, or any other inconsistencies herein. This publication is meant as a source of valuable information for the reader; however, it is not meant as a replacement for direct expert assistance. If such level of assistance is required, the services of a competent professional should be sought.

Unless otherwise indicated, all the characters in this book are fictitious. Any resemblance to actual persons, living or dead, is purely coincidental.

Disclaimers

The publisher and the author are providing this book and its contents on an "as is" basis and make no representations or warranties of any kind with respect to this book or its contents. The publisher and the author disclaim all such representations and warranties, including but not limited to warranties of healthcare for a particular purpose. In addition, the publisher and the author assume no responsibility for errors, inaccuracies, omissions, or any other inconsistencies herein.

The content of this book is for informational purposes only and is not intended to diagnose, treat, cure, or prevent any condition or disease. You understand that this book is not intended as a substitute for consultation with a licensed practitioner. Please consult with your own physician or healthcare specialist regarding the suggestions and recommendations made in this book. The use of this book implies your acceptance of this disclaimer.

The publisher and the author make no guarantees concerning the level of success you may experience by following the advice and strategies contained in this book, and you accept the risk that results will differ for each individual. The testimonials and examples provided in this book show exceptional results, which may not apply to the average reader and are not intended to represent or guarantee that you will achieve the same or similar results.

To all the parents who needed guidance
after their loss and didn't have it.

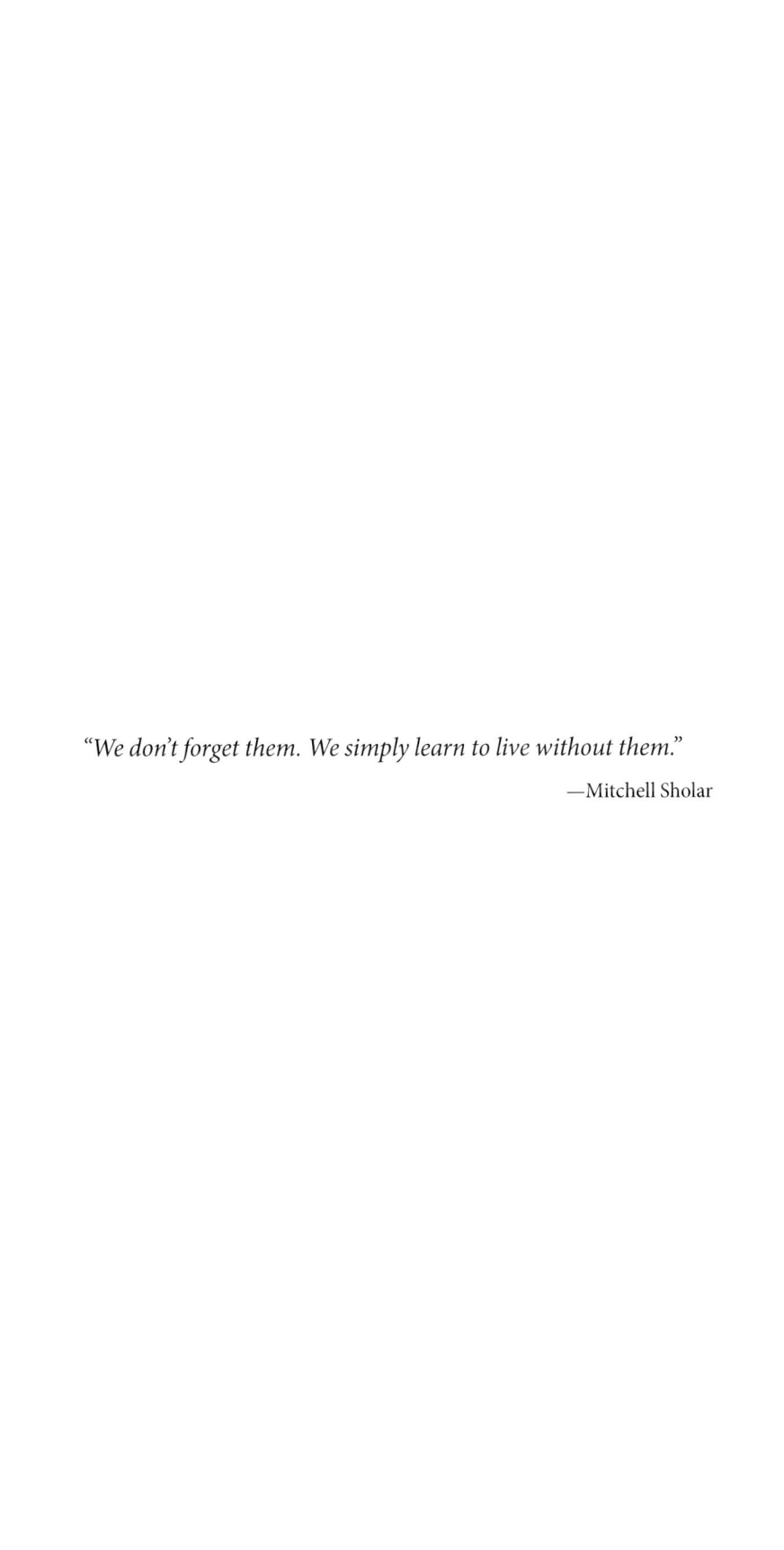

"We don't forget them. We simply learn to live without them."

—Mitchell Sholar

Table of Contents

Preface 1

Acknowledgments 5

Introduction 7

PART ONE: FILLING IN THE BLANKS

1. The Administrative Side of Loss 12
   - Reporting and Other Options 14
   - Final Arrangements 16
   - A Follow-Up Appointment 21

2. Why Did This Happen? 28
   - Types of Loss and Contributing Factors 30
   - Pregnancy after a Loss 38
   - Prevention 39
   - Glossary Of Pregnancy Loss Terminology with Definitions 41

3. Unique Challenges of Parenthood: Recovering Your Identity (And Your Body) 45
   - Recovering Your Identity 47
   - Recovering Your Body after a Loss 49

4. Now What? *Coming to Terms* 58
   - Coming to Terms 59
   - What to Do with the Nursery, Gifts, and Other Items 62
   - Shaping your narrative 70

PART TWO: FINDING RESILIENCE

5. Coping Well — 78
- Understanding Grief — 78
- Grief Reactions — 83
- Coping Skills, Strategies, and Actions — 86

6. The Partner-Parent Perspective: Being Support*ed* and Being Support*ive* — 94
- Supporting the Supporter—*Taking Care of Yourself* — 95
- Understanding Your Support Needs — 100
- Coping with Incongruent Grief — 101
- Supporting Your Partner — 104

7. Sharing the News with Others — 109
- Is sharing the news right for you? — 110
- Preparing to Deliver the News — 115
- What to Say and How to Say It—to Adults — 116
- Managing People's Reactions — 118
- What to Say and How to Say It—to Children — 120

PART THREE: LEARNING TO LIVE WITHOUT THEM: NAVIGATING LIFE WHILE COPING

8. Accepting ~~Help~~ Support — 130
- Defining Your Circle and Ways They Can Support You — 131
- Getting Support When You Don't Have a Support Network — 134
- Accepting Support from a Professional — 136

9. Grief Triggers — 142
- Five Types of Grief Triggers — 144
- Navigating Grief Triggers — 150

10. Self-Care 156
- Five Types of Self-Care 157

11. Goal-Setting 173
- Benefits of Goal-Setting 173
- Achieving Goals with a Vision Board 175

Conclusion 182

Bibliography 185

Preface

On October 8th, 1996, I was in the backseat of an '89 Lincoln Continental, watching the street whiz by as we raced through red lights to get to the hospital. My baby was breech, and his feet had just slipped down out of my body. I was only five and a half months pregnant. I was in shock, too stunned to speak or even cry anymore.

My consciousness started to fade from blood loss, and I remember only random moments after that. The vehicle came to a stop. A pack of nurses appeared. Elevator doors opened. I was in a bed, being told to push, being told not to push. A baby was placed on my chest. I was told his organs weren't developed enough for him to survive outside my body. I saw his heart beating, then no longer saw his heart beating. The next day, people stared at me as I was wheeled through the hallways and put into the back seat of that blood-stained '89 Lincoln Continental to go home.

At home, I sat on the edge of my bed, wondering what just happened. It felt like I had just been chucked out of a roaring tornado. One minute I was planning how to raise my baby. And the next, I was sorting through the wreckage to piece my broken world back together.

Now what? I couldn't go back to my life the way it was before; I was a changed person. I also couldn't go forward into the future I had planned with my baby. So what was I supposed to do? *How could I move forward when I was leaving something so precious behind? What was wrong with my body that would cause something like this? Are feelings this intense normal . . . or am I just crazy or too weak to handle what happened to me?* I had nowhere to go with my questions or my pain.

Eventually, I gave up on trying to find answers and validation. Instead, I chose to avoid thinking about the experience altogether. I didn't know what else to do. So, I left it behind in the rearview mirror of that '89 Lincoln Continental.

Twenty-two years passed, and I got married to a wonderful husband. After months of trying for a baby, I found out I was pregnant. This was especially exciting because this would be the first time my pregnancy wasn't connected to trauma. Then out of the blue, the tornado struck again. I had a miscarriage. There I was again, sitting on the edge of my bed, wondering what just happened.

I remembered all the questions I had after my first loss that never got answers. I knew the heavy toll those unanswered questions could have, so I tried not to think about them. I figured if I had gotten through it before, I could somehow do it again. People often say, "Time heals all wounds," and I had held onto that as my only source of guidance. But I started to realize that this wasn't true for me. Even after twenty-two years, the pain was still there. Time didn't heal me then and wouldn't heal me now. But what would?

I didn't know the answer but was desperate to figure it out.

My first stop in search of healing was therapy. I unloaded all the years of frustration, anger, grief, and questions I'd pent up. Therapy helped me see that I wasn't weak or crazy for the feelings I was having. I was simply a mom grieving the loss of her baby. I now had a safe space to express myself to someone who understood what I was going through.

I told people in my group of friends and family about what happened to me and found that some of them also had losses that they kept hidden. We talked about similar challenges and how things would have been easier to manage if we had gotten specific answers and guidance sooner. Being part of a community of people who had gone through the same things as I did gave me a sense of belonging and shooed away the lonely feeling.

In my continued search for healing, I was learning a lot about loss, grief, and coping, and it took consistent practice to keep all the lessons I was learning at play. I decided to write everything down to keep track and quickly reference it whenever I needed to. That's when I remembered I had this blank notebook my niece gave me. She was here visiting for Christmas and drew this beautifully detailed artwork on the outside of the notebook and wrote this thoughtful message on the inside:

To: My aunt

I love you so much. Always write in this notebook when you have an idea, no matter how small or bold. I promise it will grow into something amazing. I love you always.

Love, Sage

Whenever I learned something that helped me see a little more light of day, I wrote it in this notebook that ultimately became The Pregnancy Loss Guidebook.

This book initially started as a personal pursuit toward healing but has now expanded into a larger mission to share guidance and valuable information with other parents after loss. I hope this resource, created with you in mind, positively impacts your path to coping with your pregnancy or infant loss. I'm so honored to share it with you and be part of your support community.

— *Monica Sholar Anderson*

Acknowledgments

I am deeply grateful for the many people who supported me in writing *The Pregnancy Loss Guidebook*.

Thank you to my husband, Steven, for listening to me for hours as I processed my own experiences and for encouraging me to create this resource to help others do the same. You held my hand through the difficult process of writing and rewriting, and you made sure I took breaks when I needed them.

Thank you to my son, Justin, for always popping his head in my office to read a paragraph or chapter and provide feedback. Your perspective as someone who has lived through pregnancy loss from a child's view was invaluable.

Thank you to the team of folks who reviewed and gave input on the material:

(Community/Peers) Tayler Jones, Lauren Rosenberg, Gina McGarey, Tamesha Rouse, Eden Sabolboro, and Tiffany King.

(Industry professionals) Brandy Mason, Elizabeth Goudie, LaTresa Wiley, Melisa Scott, Kayla Holbein, Aimee Vantine, Michelle Nie, and Irv Leon. Your input was instrumental in shaping the book.

Special thanks to Dr. Rosalyn Maben-Feaster for your medical review.

Thank you to all the parents and medical providers who shared their experiences with pregnancy loss in interviews, focus groups, and needs assessment surveys. You courageously opened up about deeply personal experiences to help others. This book would not have been possible without your perspectives.

Thank you to the Remembering Cherubs Board of Directors and volunteers for your partnership and support of my work. You have been champions for this cause and for this book from the beginning.

Thank you to my family and friends for your encouragement and love throughout this process. You lifted me up on the hard days and cheered me on every step of the way.

And thank you to my angel babies. You inspire me every day to find purpose and meaning in the work I do to support families like ours. This book is written in your honor.

Introduction

Even after two losses, I still didn't know what to do next or where to turn for direction. The hospital gave me only a stuffed animal and a thin pamphlet to read. Nothing showed me how to adjust to this new version of life. Sadly, many grieving parents face this same reality after a loss—they don't have the information they need to move forward.

Stuffed animals and pamphlets may bring a moment of comfort and clarity in the immediate aftermath of a loss. Still, they don't provide lasting answers or guidance through the unique situations parents face—things nobody prepares you for, like handling precious remains, sharing the news of your loss, or managing baby shower gifts that are no longer needed.

Parents deserve to have detailed information on coping with these unique challenges. I've found answers to common questions and a path that made me feel whole again. In this book, I'll share this insight and guide you on tried and true ways to cope well and find your path to healing.

Healing is the process of having an emotional wound close more and more so you can function and live a full life despite the profound impact of your loss. Keep in mind that healing isn't a destination. It's a constant state of applying the tools and coping skills you'll learn in this book as you continue forward.

It took me over two decades to piece together some helpful information that led to better days. I don't want anyone else to go through the same struggles I did to get there—searching for answers on the Internet only to find non-working links, seeking validation from sources that didn't have the answers, or ignoring my feelings because I didn't know what else to do with them.

In this guidebook, I wanted to offer information about situations people commonly face when coping with loss. To do this, I needed to learn about loss from a viewpoint other than my own. So, I got together with experts—parents who have experienced loss—and hosted over a dozen focus group sessions and conducted surveys to gather their insights and perspectives. But I didn't stop there; I also held advisory sessions with professionals ranging from medical practitioners to psychologists to grief counselors to gain scientific and industry insight.

On top of that, I took classes and workshops on multiple topics like grief or health disparities to inform this guidebook. I combined all this knowledge with my research and pulled from the lived experiences of people in the loss community to create relatable and relevant content just for you.

As you read this book, I want you to feel like you're conversing with a community of friends who have been through situations similar to what you're experiencing and who are offering perspectives on coping that worked for them and could work for you. So you will notice that the narrative voice I used when writing the chapters is "we." This narration style serves to remind you that many people contributed to this guidebook to help guide your path. And we're all rooting for you.

Throughout the chapters, you'll find personal stories and quotes inspired by true events from my life and others within the loss community. These stories are there to provide insight in a relatable and non-clinical way.

The first part of this book will fill in the blanks on administrative expectations, the contributing factors to loss, and the unique challenges parents face.

Part two will help you tap into your resilience with tips and guidance on how to cope, be a supportive partner (while being supported), and share the news of the loss in ways you're comfortable with.

Finally, the book wraps up with part three, which focuses on navigating life while coping with loss. You'll learn about three main types of support and where to access them, overcoming grief triggers, and caring for your whole self even on those hard-to-get-out-of-bed days.

I hope that by following the guidance laid out for you, you will finally have the answers you've been looking for and be on your way to coping well.

Join me on this guided journey toward healing—a journey that is unique for each of us (and sometimes has potholes and rough terrain) but one that we can navigate together.

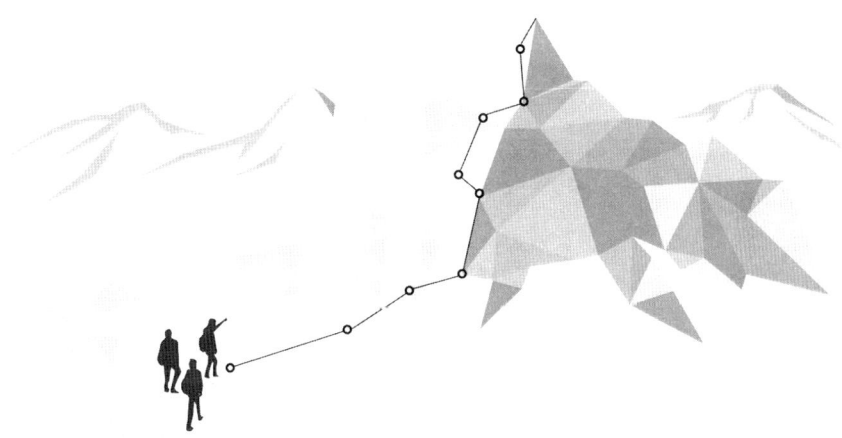

Part One
Filling In The Blanks

Chapter 1
The Administrative Side of Loss

Here are some terms to help you better navigate this chapter:

Early Loss: Early loss, also known as a miscarriage, occurs when a pregnancy ends before thirteen completed weeks.

Embryo/Fetus: After conception, the developing baby is called an embryo until it reaches eight weeks of development. At this point, it's referred to as a fetus until it's born.

Gestation: Gestation refers to the period of time between conception and birth. It describes how far along the pregnancy is.

Infant Death: Infant death is the death of a baby in the first year of life. It includes neonatal death (within twenty-eight days of birth) and post-neonatal death (after twenty-eight days but before one year).

Termination of a Desired Pregnancy for Maternal Health or Fetal Anomaly: This refers to the termination of a pregnancy due to medical reasons that threaten the health, survival, or quality of life of the baby or the person carrying it.

Miscarriage: Miscarriage is a spontaneous, unintended loss of pregnancy before the twentieth week of gestation.

Stillbirth: Stillbirth is a term used to describe the death of a fetus in the womb, generally after twenty weeks of gestation. It occurs in approximately one in 175 US births each year. It is also referred to by other names such as intrauterine death, fetal demise, and fetal death.

When my first baby was stillborn, I felt completely and utterly robbed. Before I could even begin to process my grief and seek closure, I had to take care of unexpected administrative decisions and forms that made me feel incredibly overwhelmed when I was already in such a vulnerable state. There were certain questions I should have asked, but I didn't know what I didn't know. It was hard to think straight during a time when all I wanted to do was grieve. There is a lot I wish I had known then that I know now.

—Lorena, 64

After a pregnancy or infant loss, whether it happened in the emergency room, in the hospital, or at home, you may need to consider several aspects of the administrative process. Grief often complicates these matters, making them emotionally taxing. But gaining a basic understanding can help make the administrative side of loss easier to get through.

This chapter will shed light on the administrative side of loss and everything that comes with it. We cover the basics, from the differences between live birth and fetal death to getting birth and death certificates, naming your child, and final arrangements. We also touch on the importance of your follow-up appointments. Whether you have experienced a loss or are preparing for one, this chapter has helpful information.

Reporting and Other Options

There's an important distinction between live birth and fetal death. This section will explain why it matters from an administrative and personal point of view to help you make informed decisions.

The definition of **live birth** varies in different states. To make it easier to abide by domestic laws, doctors often define a live birth as when an infant displays any evidence of life after delivery, such as breath, a pulse, or an active umbilical cord. The parents fill out paperwork to report the live birth to the state, and a birth certificate is issued. When a baby is born alive and then dies, parents usually work with a funeral home director to get the death certificate from their county clerk's office.

You have the choice to get your live-born baby a social security number. It could give you advantages when filing taxes since you can claim the child as a dependent in their birth and death year. We'd encourage you to look into this further by visiting the Social Security Administration website. They have lots of information on eligibility requirements and helpful guides.

Fetal death is when a fetus dies at any time during pregnancy and doesn't show signs of life after birth. Stillbirth falls under the category of fetal death. According to data from the Centers for Disease Control and Prevention (CDC), most states require that medical providers officially report a fetal death after twenty weeks of pregnancy. Reporting means they record it with the state. Unfortunately, losses before the twenty-week mark are usually not formally reported. That said, certain states report losses at all gestation periods to recognize all forms of fetal loss. Check the rules in your state by visiting the CDC website.

Many people feel a sense of injustice when they learn that their state doesn't report fetal deaths until a certain gestation period. What matters most is how you choose to honor and remember your baby. The reporting system of government agencies does not give or take away from the importance of your baby's life. There isn't a threshold for when we acknowledge and grieve for someone we have lost. From embryo to infant, every life carries undeniable weight in the heart of the people who loved them.

Loss due to termination for maternal health or fetal anomaly is not considered fetal death. And the implications and legal requirements for each can differ. Some states have laws that prohibit any pregnancy termination. Consult with a healthcare provider or legal expert in your state to determine the specific laws and regulations regarding terminations.

Here are some clarifications to remember:

- Live-born babies can get birth and death certificates and a social security number.
- Babies who die due to fetal death (stillbirth) do not get birth or death certificates. Parents can apply with the state to get a certificate of stillbirth. In most states, a formal record of the loss is made in cases of loss after twenty weeks of gestation.
- Pregnancies lost due to miscarriage are not eligible to receive birth, death, or stillbirth certificates. Very few states make a formal record of the loss.
- Pregnancies lost due to termination for maternal health or fetal anomaly are not eligible to receive birth, death, or stillbirth certificates. Providers formally report the loss to the state in states where pregnancy termination is legal.

After a loss, families often want to make decisions about how to honor and remember the life of their lost child. There are many options for ancillary services or rituals that may bring comfort to grieving parents. Capturing a baby's footprints or having a professional photographer take photos of your baby are two examples of services you can take advantage of. Some hospitals have cooling mats or cots available to parents so they can extend their precious time with their babies. There may also be spiritual or religious rituals, such as blessings or baptisms, performed by hospital staff. Any service or ceremony should honor your beliefs. You can decide what suits you and your family.

You may find yourself in a confusing situation regarding naming your baby. It can be hard to know when and how to name a baby you lost before you had a chance to meet them; yet it can be a meaningful choice for grieving parents. If the sex of the baby is unknown, some parents refer to their baby as "Baby Wilson" or whatever name feels true to them. You may even find solace in allowing your baby to exist without identity if that's your preference. No matter what, you have permission to find healing in whatever feels best for you. Keep in mind that in cases where a death record is formally reported, if you decide not to give your baby a name, you may not be able to change your mind later. Additionally, once the state records the name, you may not be able to change it at a later time. Check with the vital records department for your state to be sure.

Grieving parents may worry that they will never be able to find closure without an explanation for what caused the loss. In some cases, a post-mortem exam may be possible to understand any contributing factors to the death. Also referred to as an autopsy, doctors or social workers can let you know if this is an option and fill you in on how the process works and what type of results to expect.

Now that we understand reporting and other options better, the next section will help us understand our choices for final arrangements for babies lost at any stage of pregnancy.

Final Arrangements

In many states, when a baby is live-born but dies or dies due to fetal death, a funeral home must be involved in handling the remains for cremation or burial. Though most hospitals have a preferred vendor for these cases, you also have the option to choose your own funeral home. In cases involving early loss, cremation and burial are often not options because there is not enough bone matter to produce cremated remains or tissue to perform a burial.

Be advised that some hospitals place a hold on fetal and infant remains before they can be released for cremation or burial. Upon an infant's death, medical professionals follow a rigorous protocol. This often includes an autopsy to determine the cause of death, especially in cases of sudden unexpected infant deaths (SUIDs). The remains are then preserved until they can be released to the family. The legal frameworks governing the release of fetal and infant remains vary by jurisdiction, but they typically require hospitals to keep the remains for a certain period before releasing them. This is done to ensure that all necessary medical and legal procedures have been completed, including autopsies, examinations, and investigations, if required. Some faiths have specific rites and rituals for dealing with remains. In these cases, parents should communicate with their hospital to try to accommodate any special requests.

Fetal remains from a loss due to termination for maternal health or fetal anomaly are handled differently in each state. The laws and regulations vary greatly, as states have different policies on this issue. In some states, regulations require fetal remains to be cremated or buried, and the healthcare facility may cover the cost. Other states may have less specific guidelines on how fetal remains should be handled, leaving it up to the individual or the healthcare facility to determine the final arrangements. Regardless of the laws in each state, healthcare providers are required to handle fetal remains with sensitivity and respect.

Many states and hospitals understand the financial burden families face and offer assistance options to help cover the cost of burial or cremation. The best place to start is with your hospital social worker or nurse, who will have information on available resources. Additionally, many organizations offer financial aid for this very purpose. If you're at a loss for where to turn, do a simple Internet search for "burial assistance for babies" and consider what resources would be a good fit for your family. Know that there are people and organizations here to help you.

Part of the grieving process for some parents is to pay tribute to the life lost—no matter how brief—in a meaningful way. There are many creative options for honoring and remembering your child:

(Starred items are kid-sibling friendly)

- Get a tattoo
- *Create a personalized birth certificate or value-of-life certificate
- *Create a memory box or scrapbook with sonograms, photos, hospital bracelets, or other items that hold special meaning
- *Plant a tree or flower in your baby's memory
- *Have a piece of jewelry made with your baby's birthstone
- *Light a candle in your baby's memory
- *Write a letter to your baby
- Donate to a research fund for pregnancy loss or infant death
- Volunteer your time to support other families who have experienced pregnancy loss or infant death

October is recognized as Pregnancy and Infant Loss Awareness Month, a significant period dedicated to raising awareness about issues such as miscarriage, stillbirth, and infant loss. Initiated by President Ronald Reagan in 1988, this month holds profound importance as it helps families openly discuss their experiences, eliminating the stigma that often surrounds these losses. On October 15th, Pregnancy and Infant Loss Remembrance Day is observed, highlighting the critical role of community support in the grieving process. One of the most poignant events during this day is the International Wave of Light, where families across the globe light candles at 7:00 p.m. local time in memory of their lost babies. We encourage you to attend local memorial activities or hold a private ceremony to honor and remember your child.

Most people know about donating organs like the heart, kidney, or liver. But few people know they can donate tissues like skin, bone, and even the placenta. Donated tissues can help people who have been burned, hurt in an accident, or have a disease. Medical researchers can also use donated tissues to find previously unavailable treatments.

Deciding to donate organs and tissues after losing an infant can be difficult for parents. Yet, knowing that their child can help people in need and support medical research can provide peace of mind. Different rules apply, and donation options may be limited. Talk to a doctor, nurse, or hospital social worker about available services and eligibility.

For a miscarriage that happens at home, you may have questions about handling remains.

> *My friend had her loss on the toilet. She called me in shambles and didn't know whether or not to flush. It's not something anyone should ever have to think about. But that was her situation. She decided to flush. When I had my loss, I was further along than she had been, so when the remains came out, I was able to collect them and take them to my doctor. Our experiences were drastically different, and neither response was right or wrong. It was just the response we chose from the unfortunate options we had.*
> —Janel, 30

While everyone's circumstances differ, you should make decisions regarding handling the remains without any self-judgment or shame. Some people flush the remains while others collect them. Both are natural choices.

How far along you were in the pregnancy can play a big factor in what to expect of the remains and how you handle them. If you were less than eight weeks pregnant, the remains would likely be like menstrual bleeding. However, if you were past the eight-week mark up to the twenty-week mark, the remains may range in color, appear as clots, or even have a resemblance to a baby, with identifiable body parts.

Some people who collect the remains do so because they want to dispose of them in a special way, such as burial or planting in a garden. Others collect the remains to take to their doctor for an examination to try to understand why the loss happened and if there are other risk factors. These exams don't always yield answers, but many people feel it's worth trying.

If you plan to collect the remains, you'll want to use a sterile container to store them in. It can be something simple like a plastic Tupperware or a new zip-up sandwich bag. If you are collecting the remains for examination by a doctor, wear gloves like the nitrile medical gloves found at a local drugstore and wash your hands thoroughly before and after handling.

Once you have collected the remains in the container, store them in the refrigerator until you can get to your doctor or decide your plans for them. Don't freeze them, as this may cause problems with testing. Make sure to label the container with your name, the date and time, and a clear description of what's inside.

More often than not, miscarriages happen unexpectedly. But in some situations, like part of a planned procedure, some people know they will have the loss and can prepare in advance to handle the remains. If you know beforehand, ask your doctor what supplies they have to support you. Some hospitals have kits that come with collection cups and all the things you need for collection.

If you feel unsure about what's best for your situation, we suggest reaching out for direction. In addition to your doctor or nurses, hospitals often have bereavement coordinators on staff who can help assess your individual needs and give advice on how best to move forward.

Equally important to the administrative affairs that must be handled after a pregnancy or infant loss is scheduling and attending a follow-up doctor's appointment. The following section will go over expectations for your appointment and ways to prepare.

A Follow-Up Appointment

When it came time for my follow-up doctor's appointment, I had trouble articulating my questions and concerns about my health because my thoughts revolved only around the loss of my baby. I was so mired in sadness that everything else seemed unimportant. I wish I had been better prepared for the appointment. I now know how important it is to pay attention to your own needs when dealing with such profound loss.

—Maurissa, 34

Scheduling a follow-up appointment with a doctor is necessary to ensure you're making appropriate progress and getting answers to any questions. A follow-up appointment benefits your overall well-being and helps you build a strong relationship with your doctor. We strongly believe in advocating for yourself and taking the time to make sure you have the best care possible. So, even if your doctor hasn't suggested one, we recommend scheduling a follow-up appointment as soon as possible. This appointment can give you the physical and emotional support you need.

No matter how prepared you feel going in, you'll likely still have questions throughout the process, and that's normal. Having a loved one or a loss doula attend your appointment can help you feel supported and stay on track. Let's review the details that will help you to be confident and ready when your appointment arrives.

What to expect during the appointment:

A check-up: Your doctor will ask relevant questions about the circumstances surrounding your loss and any symptoms you felt afterward. They will look for signs of infection or any other physical issues that might have contributed to the loss. They may also perform an exam to ensure that all matter has passed from your womb safely.

Testing: Depending on their findings in the check-up, your doctor may order tests to check hormones or other factors. Having these tests done as soon as possible can help your doctor determine and address any underlying issues quickly.

What to do during the appointment:

Ask questions: This is your time to get answers about everything you may be wondering, from when it's safe to have sex again to whether or not you can exercise. Remember, there are no silly or dumb questions when seeking reassurance from your healthcare provider. Making a list of your questions before the appointment will help ensure that you make the most of your time with your doctor. Prioritize more significant questions first and then ask any remaining questions afterward.

Get clarity on why it happened: It's natural for parents who have gone through loss to want answers about what happened and whether it could happen again. Some people question whether having a drink of wine, taking medication, or eating certain foods contributed to their pregnancy loss. While doctors may not always be able to give you an answer, allow them to provide as much scientific knowledge as possible to clarify things for you.

Discuss any concerns or fears: Tell your doctor everything on your mind. They should have the resources and years of experience treating other patients to give knowledgeable advice. Again, make a list to prioritize what you want to say.

Acknowledge any physical pain: Describe physical pain or any discomfort you may have in as much detail as possible. A detailed description of how you feel will help the doctor determine whether you need further medical attention. If your pain is more than you can handle, don't hesitate to ask for help. Your doctor can recommend the next steps, whether that's an exam or testing or over-the-counter or prescription medications for relief. They may also suggest natural remedies or products commonly found around the house that can bring comfort.

Ask about available resources: Many health organizations provide free resources such as medication samples, educational handouts, and in-person and virtual support groups. Take advantage of these tools. They can make a big difference in helping you adjust to life moving forward. And don't forget about the power of nurses and social workers. They can be real heroes in times like these, from setting up appointments and finding resources like grieving communities or counselors to offering emotional support when needed.

Confirm understanding of your care plan: Before leaving the appointment, ensure that you fully understand both short-term and long-term goals for your recovery. Take notes, repeat back what the doctor said, and ask questions. Make sure you know any next steps or expectations from the appointment to get the most out of it. Having a support person with you can help you ensure that nothing is missed.

If you need medical care and don't have a doctor, consider visiting a community health center or free clinic. These centers usually offer treatment options with low or no fees, making them ideal for people who don't have insurance. In most cases, they accept all forms of payment so everyone can get treatment. Emergency rooms or urgent care centers generally accept patients regardless of their ability to pay. Take advantage of whatever treatment you can to ensure your body gets the care it deserves.

Conclusion

Managing the administrative side of pregnancy and infant loss can be challenging. However, understanding how reporting works and knowing your options for final arrangements and memorializing your child can make it easier. Scheduling a follow-up appointment with your doctor can also provide physical support and possibly some answers to your questions. There is no right way to go, but with knowledge and support, you can figure out the best path for you.

Rest Stop

1. **Take a moment to reflect**. Write down a lesson from this chapter that will help guide your way, like scheduling a follow-up doctor's appointment. Writing your thoughts can help you process the information you've taken in and make it easy to create a list of things you want to discuss with your doctor.

2. **Get a dedicated notebook**. We suggest using a notebook that is devoted solely to your path to coping well. A dedicated notebook lets you write down important things you want to remember. It also keeps your notes from getting lost or mixed in with other material. If you prefer to use technology, like a laptop or cellphone, that's fine too. Just make sure it has space dedicated just for this. Or, feel free to use the notes page at the end of each chapter.

3. **Take the *Crawl. Walk. Run. Soar.* self-assessment**. This self-assessment allows you to reflect on your progress in coping well after your loss and acknowledge your accomplishments.

The assessment has four separate ratings: Crawl, Walk, Run, and Soar. Each rating represents a different level of progress:

Crawling: This category represents the beginning of your healing journey. Small but determined actions are crucial in building a solid foundation for coping well. With each small action moving you forward, you are building confidence and resilience.

Walking: This category represents building momentum and making steady, consistent progress. You are no longer taking small steps but walking purposefully and gaining strength and optimism with each passing day.

Running: This category represents taking rapid strides despite challenges. You are no longer walking but running forward with conviction and determination, overcoming challenges and obstacles along the way.

Soaring: This category represents reaching new heights as you move toward an optimistic future. You have surpassed your previous limits and are soaring toward new opportunities and possibilities.

The *Crawl. Walk. Run. Soar.* self-assessment can help you identify how you are feeling and push you to keep going each day. Even if it seems insignificant, any progress is still progress. After a while, you'll be able to look back, see how far you've come, and be proud of your effort.

Remember: One day, you may soar, and the next, you may crawl. And that's okay. Healing isn't a linear journey with a set destination. It's continual progress toward feeling better.

Take the *Crawl. Walk. Run. Soar.* self-assessment:

How are you feeling today? (circle one)

Crawling – Making small but determined actions on your path to healing.

Walking – Building momentum and making steady, consistent progress.

Running – Taking rapid strides despite challenges.

Soaring – Reaching new heights as you move forward toward an optimistic future.

4. **Take a break**. We encourage you to take time to rest your mind. Studies have shown that taking breaks during learning helps improve retention and processing of information. So, step away from this book and do something you enjoy. Go for a walk, listen to music, or spend time with loved ones. Come back to the next chapter tomorrow with a refreshed mind and a renewed spirit.

Notes

Chapter 2
Why Did This Happen?

Here are some definitions to help you better navigate this chapter:

Trimester: A trimester refers to a thirteen-week (three-month) period within a pregnancy, which is divided into three distinct stages: first trimester (up to thirteen weeks and six days), second trimester (fourteen to twenty-seven weeks and six days), and third trimester (twenty-eight weeks and beyond).

Uterus: The uterus (or womb) is a hollow organ in a female's pelvis where a fetus develops and grows.

As much as I wanted to be strong and stay positive throughout my pregnancy, nothing could have prepared me for the news I got. The doctors told me it was a "miscarriage," as if I had somehow improperly carried the baby, which only added to my confusion and grief. Why did this happen? Was there something wrong with me? Why couldn't I carry a baby full term like so many other women can?

For weeks afterward, I tried desperately to find answers to those questions, searching through books and online forums for any explanation that might bring me some peace. It never seemed enough, no matter how hard I looked or what information I uncovered. At first, the questions consumed my every thought. But I couldn't continue like that; it wasn't good for my mental health.

I finally came to understand that sometimes life throws us curveballs, and we may never have a suitable answer as to why they come our way. Nowadays, I have turned my focus toward healing myself emotionally instead of trying to solve an unsolvable mystery. Day by day, peace returns to its rightful place in my heart, and I'm grateful for it—I thought I would never feel at peace again.

—Stephanie, 37

After enduring pregnancy or infant loss, many of us are left struggling for answers and asking ourselves why. Though it's natural to want to understand what happened and for what reason, we have to consider that miscarriage is a largely uncontrollable outcome and that stillbirth, infant death, and termination of a desired pregnancy can often be related to circumstances beyond our control. Acknowledging this doesn't automatically make the pain any less. Many factors can lead to these losses, and we will explore some common ones. But first, let's be clear on what are not the reasons:

- **Your worthiness**: Your loss does not indicate your worthiness to have a child. Believing that your worth as a person affects the result of your pregnancy can be very harmful to your emotional health. Know that you are worthy and valuable despite what has happened.

- **Punishment**: Experiencing a loss does not mean you have done something wrong. The loss didn't happen due to Karma or any curse. And it doesn't indicate any wrongdoings or sins on your part. Don't view it as a punishment for any past actions.

- **Your feelings**: Feeling uncertain or unready to be a parent or not being excited about the pregnancy did not cause your loss to happen.

Your feelings don't have the power to determine the outcome of your pregnancy.

A research study found that parents sometimes feel responsible for the loss, whether from their own ideas or influence from others. *I didn't eat enough; I should have exercised less; I should have been more attentive.* It's natural that we might feel accountable for the loss, particularly when there is no identifiable cause. Even in cases where there is a known cause, some parents still feel they are to blame. Hear us loud and clear: do not assign blame to yourself or your body.

In this chapter, we will examine the facts surrounding what could be to blame and what steps we can take toward prevention.

Types of Loss and Contributing Factors

Before we dive into the types of loss, we have to clarify something. The term "pregnancy loss" can be distressing for some people. It wasn't simply a pregnancy that we lost, but rather, for many of us, it was a being that we lost, a loved person—not to mention the loss of hopes and dreams for the future.

Throughout this guidebook, we use the term "pregnancy loss" simply as a catch-all phrase to refer to any pregnancy that ended in loss.

According to March of Dimes, as many as half of all pregnancies may end in miscarriage. Yes, almost half. This includes estimates of women who didn't even know they were pregnant (and likely assumed they had a late period). Like us, you may be staggered by knowing that this happens so commonly. But miscarriage is just one aspect of pregnancy loss. Pregnancy loss has three easily identifiable categories: miscarriage, stillbirth, and infant death. Sometimes doctors perform a termination to end a desired pregnancy. We think of this as a fourth category of pregnancy loss.

When we speak of pregnancy loss, our thoughts often turn to the physical loss. But let's not forget about infertility. It's a form of loss that lingers in the quiet moments, in the unfulfilled desire to have a child. And so it deserves recognition.

Each type of loss has its unique circumstances in which it tends to occur. Miscarriage, stillbirth, and infant death are typically defined by the gestational age of the pregnancy or age of the child when the loss happened. In contrast, terminations are determined by the circumstances leading to the decision.

Let's look at each loss type more closely.

Miscarriage (a spontaneous, unintended loss of pregnancy before the twentieth week of gestation)

Let's first address the insensitivity of the word "miscarriage" when referring to pregnancy loss. Many of us have been hurt or offended by medical professionals using this terminology to describe the loss of a much-desired pregnancy. The term implies fault, and the scientific phrase for it—"spontaneous abortion"—isn't much better. While we dislike using the word "miscarriage," it's necessary to address this delicate topic accurately.

Around 80 percent of miscarriages happen before the twelfth week of pregnancy. While scientists are unsure about the exact cause of every miscarriage, chromosomal abnormalities are the most common culprit. Chromosomes are threadlike structures that carry genetic information (genes) and play a crucial role in the baby's development. A chromosomal abnormality means something misfired during the baby's formation, resulting in a miscarriage. These misfires are typically chance events that doctors or parents cannot control. To be clear, miscarriage has nothing to do with your character as an individual but everything to do with biological factors.

While chromosomal abnormalities frequently cause miscarriage, they don't make up the whole picture. Several other factors contribute to miscarriages, like hormone imbalances from polycystic ovary syndrome (also known as PCOS), underlying health conditions, and infections. Racial and socioeconomic disparities in accessing appropriate healthcare are also contributing factors.

For example:

Racial Disparities: Studies have shown that Black women, and women from certain minority ethnic communities, experience significantly higher loss rates than White women and women from other racial or ethnic groups. This could be due to systemic racism in healthcare, lack of access to quality prenatal care, and higher stress levels related to racial discrimination, which may result in high-risk pregnancies (Evans, et al., 2023).

Socioeconomic Status: Lower socioeconomic status can also contribute to higher rates of loss. These individuals often have limited access to quality healthcare, face increased stress levels, and have poor nutritional status, all of which can lead to complications during pregnancy and childbirth (Turman & Swigonski, 2021).

(Race and socioeconomic status are examples of social determinants of health—the non-medical factors in the environments where people are born, live, work, and age that influence health outcomes and risks.)

White and Bouvier (2005) describe four stages of miscarriage:

Threatened Abortion: Characterized by early pregnancy vaginal bleeding without cervical dilation or change. Cramping pain or backache may occur but is typically not severe.

Inevitable Abortion: Characterized by early pregnancy vaginal bleeding with cervical dilation. Bleeding and cramping are usually more severe than with a threatened abortion, but no fetal tissue passes.

Incomplete Abortion: Characterized by vaginal bleeding during pregnancy with cervical dilation and passage of some, but not all, products of conception. Bleeding is usually heavy, and cramps are intense. An ultrasound confirms that some products of conception remain in the uterus.

Complete Abortion: Characterized by a history of vaginal bleeding, abdominal pain, and the passage of tissue. After tissue is passed, pain subsides and bleeding diminishes significantly. There should be no tenderness of the cervix, uterus, or abdomen, and an ultrasound should show an empty uterus.

Although miscarriage happens commonly, it doesn't mean your grief over it isn't justified. It can be a heartbreaking experience, and you deserve to express what you are feeling in safe ways. Chapters 8 and 10 cover tips on defining your circle of support and ways to express your emotions.

Stillbirth (the death of a fetus in the uterus after twenty weeks of gestation)

For one in three cases of stillbirth, the reasons remain unexplained. For the other two-thirds, though, potential causes may stem from a variety of different issues:

Congenital disabilities

Congenital disabilities are physical abnormalities present at birth that can impact almost any part of the body, from vital organs to extremities. They come in many forms and can be caused by genetics, environmental exposures, or drug use during pregnancy.

Infections

Infections are illnesses that occur when bacteria, viruses, or other microorganisms enter the body and cause harm. Bacterial infections in the uterus, sexually transmitted infections (STI), influenza (the flu), or infection from food contamination can lead to stillbirth.

Lifestyle choices

Lifestyle choices that include excessive alcohol consumption and recreational drug use can have serious health consequences that may lead to stillbirth.

Pre-existing diabetes

Diabetes is a chronic medical condition where the body doesn't correctly process sugar from the bloodstream, leading to high blood glucose levels. It can lead to abnormalities in maternal blood glucose levels and body mass index (BMI), potentially causing complications that could impact fetal growth and placental function.

The placenta

The placenta is the organ that forms during pregnancy where the pregnant person's and the baby's systems connect, allowing for the exchange of vital nutrients between them. Complications with the placenta can stem from conditions such as blood clotting disorders or abdominal trauma from a fall.

The umbilical cord

The umbilical cord is a structure that links the growing fetus to its mother via the placenta and serves as a crucial connection for nutrition and oxygen transfer. It can get twisted or knotted around the baby, which could cause complications. Another issue could be cord prolapse, meaning the umbilical cord slips through the cervix before the baby is born. Both can lead to stillbirth.

Infant Death (the death of an infant before their first birthday)

According to the CDC, the five leading causes of infant death are as follows:

1. **Congenital disabilities**
   Conditions like spina bifida and diaphragmatic hernia.

2. **Premature birth and low birth weight**
   Premature birth occurs before thirty-seven weeks of pregnancy, usually resulting in low birth weight (under 5 lbs 8 oz). It takes roughly forty weeks for an unborn baby to fully develop before

birth. Early-arriving infants can be much more vulnerable than full-term babies due to trouble with eating, gaining weight, and fighting off infections, which could lead to death.

3. **Sudden unexpected infant death (SUID)**

    SUID is a term used to describe the sudden and unexpected death of a baby less than one year old in which the cause wasn't clear before investigation. SUIDs include accidental suffocation while sleeping and other deaths from unknown causes, such as sudden infant death syndrome (SIDS), which is the unexplained death, usually during sleep, of a seemingly healthy baby less than a year old. SIDS is commonly known as "crib death" because the infants often die in cribs. Research has indicated that this condition might have something to do with defects in parts of the baby's brain that control breathing during sleep.

4. **Injuries**

    Causes of injury range from car crashes, drowning, poisoning, fires, and falls.

5. **Maternal pregnancy complications**

    A range of health issues, such as anemia, urinary tract infections, hypertension (high blood pressure), diabetes, and various infections, may lead to increased vulnerability during pregnancy and infant death.

Termination of a Desired Pregnancy for Maternal Health or Fetal Anomaly

A termination for maternal health refers to the termination of a pregnancy due to medical reasons that threaten the life or health of the pregnant person. These reasons may include but are not limited to pulmonary hypertension, ectopic pregnancy, or severe preeclampsia.

A termination for fetal anomaly refers to the termination of a pregnancy due to medical reasons that threaten the life or health of the baby or greatly impact their quality of life. These reasons may include but are not limited to neural tube defects and congenital heart defects.

We must highlight that a termination is not considered a fetal death. In a fetal death, the fetus dies inside the pregnant person's uterus or during childbirth. In contrast, a termination is a procedure that medical professionals perform to terminate the pregnancy before the fetus reaches full term.

You should know that the medical terminology for a termination is called an "abortion." Terminations for maternal health or fetal anomaly are not elective procedures in a traditional sense. A traditional elective abortion is when a pregnant person ends a pregnancy because they want to, not because of health reasons. In comparison, a termination for maternal health is an intervention recommended by medical professionals with concern for the pregnant person, where serious medical issues threaten their health or survival. And a termination for fetal anomaly is a decision made by parents with concern for the baby where medical issues threaten their health, survival, or quality of life.

Termination of a desired pregnancy for maternal health or fetal anomaly, unfortunately, doesn't get the recognition it deserves as a type of pregnancy loss.

The decision to terminate a pregnancy is typically made by the pregnant person and their family, in consultation with a medical team consisting of obstetricians, neonatologists, genetic counselors, and other healthcare providers, after carefully considering all available options and the potential risks. It's a difficult decision for everyone involved, where logic and emotion often conflict.

The topic of termination for maternal health or fetal anomaly is complicated, with varying medical and ethical views. It is considered a taboo and is frowned upon by many. While others, like the American College of

Obstetricians & Gynecologists, feel that "The science of medicine is not subjective, and a strongly held personal belief should never outweigh scientific evidence, override standards of medical care, or drive policy that puts a person's health and life at risk."

No matter what people think, parents who decide to have a medically necessary termination have the right to grieve and mourn the loss of their child.

We previously mentioned that the medical terminology for termination is called an "abortion." Some parents who may not identify their choice in the same manner as a traditional, elective abortion may take offense or feel distressed by the use of this language to describe the loss of their desired pregnancy. Parents should be prepared for this possibility, especially when reviewing medical documents. Such documents often use medical terminology not written in language sensitive to each individual's experience.

There are three common ways that doctors perform terminations of a desired pregnancy:

- **Via medication** – The pregnant person takes medication orally or vaginally to cause the termination. This type of termination typically occurs with pregnancies of up to nine or ten weeks' gestation.

- **Via procedure** – This requires a doctor to remove the baby surgically. An example of such a procedure is dilation and evacuation (D&E). This procedure is mostly used in the second trimester and may require sedation or anesthesia.

- **Via induction of labor** – In this case, medication is given to induce a vaginal birth. This type of termination occurs with pregnancies in the second trimester onward.

Some parents face the difficult situation of knowing that their baby will not survive outside the womb due to lethal fetal anomalies but continue the pregnancy, nevertheless. This may be due to the possibility of holding their child and spending some time together before their baby passes away. For other parents, the decision not to terminate may align with their beliefs or religious views. Each situation is unique and personal, and parents have the right to make the decision that they feel is the best choice for themselves and their families. Perinatal hospice is a service available at certain hospitals that support these families throughout the pregnancy, delivery, and post-partum period.

Pregnancy after a Loss

You should know that after a loss, many people go on to have healthy babies in the future. These babies are fondly referred to by some as "rainbow babies," likened to a rainbow appearing in the sky after a storm. Before considering plans for conceiving again, please allow yourself adequate time and space to heal from your present loss. It's understandable to want to try again right away. However, it's essential to check in with yourself and really focus on healing your emotional wounds before making such a big decision.

After a loss, some people think that having another baby will help them heal. Even friends and loved ones casually suggest trying again to avoid dealing with your present grief. But we want you to know that having another baby won't replace the one you've lost and shouldn't be presented as a remedy for your pain. There's no substitute for healing from such deep hurt; we must give ourselves time and grace to process our grief.

Focusing on yourself first will help you make any future decisions regarding parenting with clarity so that you are ready for it in the best way possible, no matter what direction life takes next—baby or not. The World Health Organization suggests waiting six months to allow your body to heal physically. While it may not always be possible to have ample space between experiencing a loss and trying again (due to circumstances like fertility concerns), it's important to remember that you have the right to take whatever amount of time you need.

Prevention

Being proactive with your health during pregnancy helps support the best possible outcome. That's why it's essential to regularly visit a doctor who can help identify and respond to any underlying conditions or risk factors that could lead to loss. Avoiding smoking, drinking alcohol, and using drugs will give you a better chance to prevent a loss from happening. Also, having a doula present throughout pregnancy and during labor and delivery can lead to positive outcomes for the baby and the person carrying it. Seeking culturally sensitive care that respects and acknowledges a person's unique experiences and advocating for policy changes that address systemic racism and socioeconomic disparities in healthcare can reduce loss rates in the long run.

Even if you do all the right things, it's still possible for a loss to happen. Don't take on the burden of blame. It's best to focus your energy on healing and coping with the loss, which you can control, rather than fretting about things you can't change—and didn't cause.

Even though we know that the common causes of pregnancy loss aren't our fault, it can still feel like we are responsible. Dismiss these types of thoughts as soon as they pop up. Dwelling on guilty feelings or blame will only hinder forward progress and make things worse. Moving forward doesn't mean you are leaving your baby in the past. It means you remember your baby but are finding healthy ways to live without them here physically. Later in this book, we will go over ways to do just that.

Conclusion

Remember: Miscarriage is a pregnancy loss that occurs between zero and twenty weeks of gestation. Stillbirth is loss after twenty weeks but before birth. Infant death is loss after a live birth through one year of age, and a termination for maternal health or fetal anomaly can occur any time during pregnancy, up to the third trimester, depending on the state law in which it occurs.

When a pregnancy or infant loss happens, it's natural to want to know why. But we shouldn't seek answers to blame ourselves. Instead, we should learn more about the loss and understand that some things are out of our control. As you do so, show yourself grace, care for your body, and set your mind on moving forward. And don't forget: before conceiving again, allow yourself the necessary time and space to heal. Your well-being is worth the wait.

At the end of this chapter, you can find a glossary of words and definitions to learn more about the different types of pregnancy loss.

Rest Stop

1. **Take a moment to reflect**. Write down a lesson from this chapter that will help guide your way, like not blaming yourself for what happened.

2. **Do a listening activity.** "Even For A Day" is a spoken-word poem set to music. It speaks to the complex range of emotions people experience after losing a baby or pregnancy. The song encourages us to explore hard questions and find ways to heal and move forward. Go to www.rememberingcherubs.org/even-for-a-day to listen to this song written and performed by *The Pregnancy Loss Guidebook* author Monica Sholar Anderson.

3. **Take the *Crawl. Walk. Run. Soar.* self-assessment**:

    How are you feeling today? (circle one)

    Crawling – Making small but determined actions on your path to healing.

Walking – Building momentum and making steady, consistent progress.

Running – Taking rapid strides despite challenges.

Soaring – Reaching new heights as you move forward toward an optimistic future.

Remember: One day, you may soar, and the next, you may crawl. And that's okay. Healing isn't a linear journey with a set destination. It is continual progress toward feeling better.

4. **Take a break**. Give your mind a well-deserved break, then come back fresh and ready to dive into the next chapter tomorrow.

Glossary Of Pregnancy Loss Terminology with Definitions

Please note there may be additional types of pregnancy loss not listed here.

Blighted Ovum: Also called an anembryonic pregnancy, it occurs when an early embryo never develops or stops developing, is reabsorbed, and leaves an empty gestational sac.

Cervical Insufficiency Causing Preterm Delivery: A medical condition in which the cervix dilates too early, resulting in pregnancy loss or premature birth.

Chemical Pregnancy: A very early miscarriage within the first five weeks of pregnancy. An embryo may form and even embed in the uterus lining, but then it stops developing.

Complete Miscarriage: When all pregnancy tissue has passed from the womb.

Dilation & Curettage (D&C): A procedure usually performed in early miscarriages using a curette to remove pregnancy tissue and fetal matter from the dilated uterus.

Dilation & Extraction (D&E): This procedure is usually performed in miscarriages after the first trimester and involves the use of forceps to take the fetus out of a dilated uterus.

Ectopic Pregnancy: In an ectopic pregnancy, the fetus develops outside the uterus, such as in a fallopian tube, the cervix, or the pelvis or abdomen. It is considered a medical emergency that cannot proceed normally since the fetus cannot survive outside the uterus. If left untreated, it may cause life-threatening bleeding in the pregnant person.

Embryonic Pregnancy: An embryonic pregnancy occurs when a fertilized egg does not develop into an embryo.

Failed In-Vitro Fertilization Cycle (IVF): IVF is a medical procedure in which an egg is fertilized by sperm outside the body. A failed cycle may be due to poor embryo/egg quality and age, poor ovarian response, or implantation dysfunction.

Hebdomadal Death: A term used to describe the death of an infant from zero to six days old, typically caused by congenital malformation or injury sustained at birth.

Incomplete Miscarriage: When a miscarriage begins, but some pregnancy tissue stays in the womb.

Induction of Labor: When medication is given to induce a vaginal birth. This occurs with pregnancies in the second trimester onward.

Infant Death, a.k.a. Infant Mortality: The death of an infant before their first birthday.

Infertility: A reproductive system issue that results in the inability to produce a pregnancy after one year or more of unprotected sex.

Termination of a Desired Pregnancy for Maternal Health or Fetal Anomaly: When parents terminate a desired pregnancy due to complications that threaten the health, survival, or quality of life of the baby or the person carrying it.

Medically Induced Miscarriage: Non-surgical treatment, which involves taking medication to induce cramping in the uterus to expel any fetal matter or pregnancy tissue.

Miscarriage: Miscarriage, also known as spontaneous abortion, is an unintended loss of pregnancy before the twentieth week of gestation.

Missed Miscarriage: When a doctor diagnoses a miscarriage without any visible signs (e.g., bleeding or cramping) based on laboratory results or other clinical evidence.

Molar Pregnancy: A condition where the placenta and fetal tissues do not develop normally.

Neonatal Infant Loss: The death of a newborn younger than twenty-eight days old, often caused by prematurity or congenital disabilities.

Recurrent Miscarriage: When a miscarriage happens three or more times in a row.

Reproductive Loss: The experience of miscarriage, stillbirth, infant death, maternal death, and the loss of a "normal" reproductive experience due to infertility or assisted reproduction.

Septic Miscarriage: Miscarriage due to an infection in the uterus.

Stillbirth: The death of a fetus in the uterus after twenty weeks of gestation.

Surrogacy Loss: A term used to describe the unsuccessful attempts of a surrogate to give birth to an intended parent's baby. It can include reproductive loss, such as miscarriage or stillbirth.

Vanishing Twin Syndrome: When a multiple pregnancy, such as twins or triplets, results in the loss of one fetus. The pregnant person and the surviving embryos absorb the tissue of the lost baby.

Notes

Chapter 3
Unique Challenges of Parenthood: Recovering Your Identity (And Your Body)

After my miscarriage, I felt so broken. Not only had I lost something so precious but also, because of my immigrant family's cultural beliefs that grieving such an early loss was unnecessary, nobody around me seemed to acknowledge or understand how impactful this was for me. Everyone just expected me to carry on as if nothing had happened. In addition to what my body was going through, I was battling questions of whether or not I was even a mother since I had conceived but had no baby to love or raise. The people around me made me feel like I was crazy for even trying to explore or get answers to what I felt were reasonable questions. "Just move on" was their view. I was surrounded by people who love me, yet I had never felt more alone in my life.

—Sunita, 26

Parenthood can be a complex journey for families, with many figures who may fill the traditional mold of "parent." From mothers and fathers to step-parents, uncles, and other caretakers, each family unit looks different in its own way. This chapter will explore unique challenges that gestational and surrogate parents face from a perspective of how loss may impact their bodies and self-image. But first, let's dive into understanding these often overlooked yet essential parental components.

Gestational Parent (or Carrier): The gestational parent is the individual who has the physical responsibility of carrying a pregnancy and giving birth. They could either be a genetic parent, meaning that their egg contributed to the pregnancy, or they could be a surrogate.

Surrogate: A surrogate is a person who carries a pregnancy for another individual or couple, giving birth to the baby on behalf of the intended parents. Surrogacy is growing in popularity as an option for people who would otherwise be unable to conceive due to infertility, a non-functioning uterus, a medical condition that puts them at significant medical risk if they become pregnant, or recurrent pregnancy loss.

Surrogacy has many types of arrangements: traditional surrogacy, where the carrier's own biological material contributes to the embryo creation; gestational surrogacy, where donor eggs are used and the carrier has no genetic relation to the child; commercial surrogacy, where there is payment involved; and altruistic surrogacy, where there is no payment but there may still be reimbursement of expenses incurred by the carrier during their pregnancy.

Genetic Parent: A genetic parent is a person who contributes either an egg or sperm to create an embryo. Multiple individuals can contribute to creating an embryo through various assisted reproductive technologies like in-vitro fertilization (IVF). They could be the intended parent who plans to raise and support the child or someone else, such as anonymous egg or sperm donors.

Intended Parent: An intended parent is someone who takes responsibility for raising and supporting a child as a physical caretaker and financial provider for a child's needs. Intended parents can include genetic parents, adoptive parents, and more. Intended parents may also be single individuals or couples, regardless of their sexual orientation.

While we recognize parenthood in these technical contexts, parenthood is often more complicated than a technical definition. Many people form strong emotional bonds with children, even before their birth, and it's not uncommon for them to consider themselves a parent even if they don't necessarily meet any of these definitions in a strict sense.

No matter what type of parenting situation is at play, we should recognize that loss can impact all parties involved in many different ways. This chapter will identify unique challenges that gestational and surrogate parents may face with their identity and from their bodies after a loss. You may not be a gestational or surrogate parent, but read this chapter anyway; there is still valuable information that you can learn from.

Recovering Your Identity

A pregnancy ending in loss can leave gestational and surrogate parents feeling as if they have failed—either their partner impacted by the grief of the loss, the intended parents who had high hopes and expectations, or themselves. Complicating matters more is that the loss can create a sense of confusion, especially when it comes to defining oneself. *"Am I still a mother?"* This is a question that has no clear answer since each person experiences this role differently.

"Mother" is formally defined as the female parent of a child. Still, society might also call a person a mother due to having given birth or having adopted or raised an offspring. At its most basic level, the concept of being a mother is often associated with love, nurturing, and caretaking—which transcends DNA.

It can be a real identity crisis when the very thing we are "supposed" to achieve as women doesn't happen. It stands to reason that we might feel disappointed that our bodies didn't let us reach the goal of becoming a "mother." But we must remind ourselves that we are still valuable and a person who is strong and capable of many things. Our loss doesn't diminish our value in any way.

Trying to assign or define your maternal identity based on other people's opinions can cause confusion and internal conflict. For example, if you had a miscarriage, some people might think you are not a mother because you don't have a child physically present, but you may still feel like one. Or, if a baby wasn't biologically related to you but you planned to raise them as your own, some people may not see you as a mother because there is no blood connection. Or even if you acted as a surrogate for somebody else's baby and felt sadness and grief after losing it, some people might not understand your grief or may feel it's out of place since the baby didn't "belong" to you.

We live in a world where pregnancy and infant loss are still profoundly misunderstood, especially regarding how different cultures and religions view them. The loss is not always met with appropriate expressions of support. Long-held beliefs and attitudes toward loss can clash with your thoughts and feelings. This disconnect can be painful to contend with and may make it difficult for you to grieve openly without fearing judgment or criticism, such as in Sunita's experience. But **don't let the views and opinions of other people define how you feel about yourself or your situation**. You are entitled to shape your identity in a way that's true to you. Whether you choose to identify yourself as a "mother" or not, do so to take ownership of your self-view. Broad societal terms don't have to define you.

To keep insensitive views at arm's length while navigating your path to healing, put effort into understanding and working through your feelings first before looking elsewhere for validation. Though allyship can be a good outlet for emotional support, nothing can replace you being your own biggest supporter.

Recovering Your Body after a Loss

What your body goes through while it recovers from a loss largely depends on the gestational age of your pregnancy when your loss happened. While this may be true, no two bodies are identical; therefore, no recovery experiences will be either. So if you have well-meaning friends or loved ones telling you that you will go through *exactly* what they did, take their advice with a grain of salt.

If your loss resulted from a medical procedure, what you experience during your physical recovery may differ from someone who had a miscarriage, stillbirth, or live birth. We'll look at what a person can expect their body to go through when recovering from loss, broken down by gestational age at the time of the loss and after a procedure.

Disclaimer: *The content of this book is for informational purposes only and is not intended to diagnose, treat, cure, or prevent any condition or disease. This book is not intended as a substitute for consultation with a licensed practitioner. Please consult with your own physician or healthcare specialist regarding the suggestions and recommendations made in this book.*

First Trimester (up to thirteen weeks and six days)

- **Spotting**: This is vaginal bleeding that includes spotting small amounts of blood in your underwear or toilet tissue after wiping. It can range from light brown to bright red. This type of bleeding usually has a lighter flow than a regular menstrual cycle and may require a panty liner.
- **Mild Discomfort**: Some people experience mild discomfort in the form of cramping or pressure, similar to what they would normally experience during their menstrual cycle. This type of pain is generally rated between zero and four on a pain scale and likely won't require medication for relief.

- **Heavy Bleeding**: Heavy bleeding is a possible symptom after loss and typically happens within one to two hours after the event. You may also have clots appearing. This kind of vaginal bleeding usually requires using a sanitary napkin. The color of the blood is generally bright red and much heavier than typical spotting.

- **Fever**: The average body temperature is 98.6°F. A temperature higher than 100.4°F generally indicates fever. A fever could mean your body's immune system is fighting off an infection. If you have a fever, contact your doctor immediately for advice. Also, let them know if you are experiencing additional issues, such as a severe headache, stiff neck, shortness of breath, or other unusual signs or symptoms. They may have you come in for an examination. They may also recommend resting and drinking plenty of fluids or suggest taking over-the-counter pain relievers like Tylenol®, Motrin®, or Advil® for immediate relief.

- **Chills**: Chills can be a sign that your body is trying to regulate its core temperature. You may shiver, tremble, have chattering teeth, or goosebumps on the surface of your skin. Chills can also occur during fever episodes. If you have chills, contact your doctor immediately for advice.

- **Intense Pain**: You could numerically rate the intensity of this pain between 8 and 10 on a pain scale. If you have severe pain, contact your doctor immediately for advice. This type of pain could indicate an underlying issue that needs immediate attention. They may have you come in for an examination. They may also recommend over-the-counter or prescription medications such as opioids or nonsteroidal anti-inflammatory drugs (NSAIDs).

Second Trimester (fourteen to twenty-seven weeks and six days)

All of the expectations listed above in Trimester 1, plus:

- **Breast Swelling and Pain**: People may experience an array of painful sensations in their breast tissue, including enlargement, tenderness, throbbing, stabbing, sharp pain, burning pain, or tightness in the breast tissue, including in the nipple area. Breasts may also become firm or engorged due to milk production. These symptoms can last up to several weeks following the loss. Gently massaging your breasts and wearing a fitted and supportive bra may lessen pain or discomfort. In severe cases, you may consider consulting with a lactation specialist.

- **Return of Your Menstrual Cycle**: Menstrual cycles usually return within four to six weeks after a pregnancy loss. It could take months for your period to get back to what you consider normal. Every individual's experience will vary, but once hormone levels return to normal, your period should resume its regular course.

- **Hormonal Changes**: Pregnancy hormones drop drastically within twenty-four hours of a loss, leaving the body to adjust quickly to these changes. This sudden adjustment can cause sleeplessness, fatigue, and irritability. It may also trigger stress hormones like cortisol, impacting physical and emotional health. Eventually, your body will adjust, and hormone levels should settle back into place in time and with support from medical professionals if necessary.

- **Nausea, Vomiting, or Diarrhea**: Feeling nauseous or experiencing vomiting and diarrhea can be expected after a loss due to changes in hormone levels or possibly medications you have taken. If these side effects persist longer than a few days, you should seek medical advice as they could indicate other underlying issues, such as dehydration or infection, that require additional treatment.

Taking some simple steps can help combat these symptoms. Begin by getting plenty of rest—your body needs it to replenish energy stores. Then keep yourself hydrated with clear fluids like water, broth, or sports drinks in moderation. Use the BRAT diet—that's bananas, rice, applesauce, and toast (all foods that are easy on your stomach)—and avoid greasy/spicy foods high in fat and sugar plus dairy and caffeine products. Over-the-counter medications such as Pepto Bismol®, Imodium AD®, or Dramamine® could also bring relief.

- **Cramping**: Cramping is another symptom commonly experienced and can range from mild discomfort to intense pain. Throbbing or cramping sensations are usually felt in the abdominal area, similar to menstrual cramps. Mild symptoms should subside over time with proper care and rest. Over-the-counter pain medicine may bring relief. If you have intense pain from cramping, contact your doctor immediately for advice. This type of pain could indicate an underlying issue that needs immediate attention.

Third Trimester and Beyond (twenty-eight weeks and beyond)
All of the expectations listed above in Trimesters 1 and 2, plus:

- **Perineum Soreness**: The perineum is the area between your vagina and rectum. During labor, it stretches and can tear, or a doctor may cut it during an episiotomy, which is a small incision made at the opening of the vagina to help get your baby out. Even if you did not deliver vaginally, you may experience soreness or bruising in this area if any physical trauma occurred during labor or delivery. Feeling sore in this area for several weeks is normal, and it may take longer for total healing to happen. Taking care of the perineum through gentle cleaning and avoiding irritating soaps and creams may help to promote faster healing.

- **Afterbirth Pains**: Afterbirth pains are contractions you feel as your uterus (womb) shrinks to its regular size after pregnancy. These sensations may vary in intensity depending on individual circumstances. They will generally subside within the first few days post-loss. Severe pain should be reported to a doctor immediately, as it could indicate an underlying medical concern that needs attention.

- **Vaginal Discharge**: After a loss, your body will typically expel blood and tissue from inside the uterus. This process is called vaginal discharge or lochia. The flow may be heavier than normal for the first few days after the loss and could contain blood clots. It may be bright red or yellowish-white, depending on the time since the loss occurred. Generally speaking, it should become lighter in color over time and eventually taper off until it stops completely, which can take about a month or longer.

- **Hemorrhoids**: Hemorrhoids are swollen veins in and around the anus that can cause discomfort, pain, and bleeding. They are common during pregnancy but can also be quite common post pregnancy loss. Many people get them due to hormonal changes associated with different stages of pregnancy as well as any trauma to the area caused by pushing during labor or delivery. To help ease symptoms, you should stay hydrated, avoid straining while going to the bathroom, and use topical medications such as creams and ointments if needed to reduce inflammation, pain, and itching. Trying a sitz bath—sitting in warm water up to the hips—is a great natural option for combatting hemorrhoids.

Termination for Maternal Health or Fetal Anomaly
(can occur any time during pregnancy, up to the third trimester, depending on the state law in which it occurs)

All of the expectations listed above, plus:

- Bleeding and cramping that can last for a few days or even up to a few weeks. These symptoms can be from the uterus shedding tissue from the pregnancy.

- In addition to bleeding and cramping, you may experience nausea and vomiting due to hormonal changes in the body or medication. These symptoms may last for a few days. If you also get a fever and chills, it could mean you have an infection and should seek immediate medical attention.

- You may feel pain from the uterus returning to its pre-pregnant size. It may happen in intervals similar to menstrual cramps and increase in intensity before dissipating altogether. Many people find relief from applying heat, taking over-the-counter pain medication, and resting. If the pain becomes intense, contact a doctor immediately.

- Headaches and diarrhea can be common symptoms of hormonal changes or side effects of the medication used in the termination process. You can usually manage these symptoms with over-the-counter pain medication, but if they persist, seek medical advice.

- Vaginal discharge after pregnancy termination is normal. It can range in color from pink to black and may be mucus-like. Monitor discharge for any unusual odor or texture, as it may indicate an infection and require medical attention.

- It's common to experience fatigue after pregnancy termination from the physical and emotional stress of the experience. Resting and taking care of yourself can help.

Stay in touch with your doctor throughout your recovery and seek medical attention if any physical changes concern you.

Conclusion

We may feel like our bodies have failed us when we don't achieve "motherhood" in the manner society expects of us. But we must give ourselves grace.

We should never feel condemned for what we have endured; instead, we should celebrate our bodies simply for enduring and surviving. No matter what title we give ourselves, whether it's mother, gestational parent, or surrogate, all that matters is knowing that we have value, and how we feel about the babies we carried cannot be denied or invalidated.

Our bodies go through many stages and experiences as we physically heal from loss. Sometimes it can be challenging to know what's normal and what needs medical attention. Don't guess. If something feels off, or you have questions, contact your doctor and let them guide you. Taking these steps can get you closer to feeling healthier physically and emotionally.

Rest Stop

1. **Take a moment to reflect**. Write down a lesson from this chapter that will help guide your way, like knowing that your value is not defined by the views and opinions of others.

2. **Take the *Crawl. Walk. Run. Soar.* self-assessment:**

   How are you feeling today? (circle one)

   Crawling – Making small but determined actions on your path to healing.

   Walking – Building momentum and making steady, consistent progress.

   Running – Taking rapid strides despite challenges.

   Soaring – Reaching new heights as you move forward toward an optimistic future.

   Remember: One day, you may soar, and the next, you may crawl. And that's okay. Healing isn't a linear journey with a set destination. It is continual progress toward feeling better.

3. **Take a break**. Give your mind a well-deserved break, then come back fresh and ready to dive into the next chapter tomorrow.

Notes

Chapter 4
Now What? *Coming to Terms*

> *I've learned that coming to terms with losing my baby doesn't mean forgetting about it or trying to pretend it didn't happen. It just means accepting what's happened and finding a way forward.*
>
> —T, 29

Adjusting to an unexpected new future is not always easy. When life doesn't go according to plan, it can be challenging to grapple with—especially after a pregnancy or infant loss. We mourn the milestones we will never get to experience: the first crawl across the playroom floor, hearing their first "Hi, Mama," watching them giggle with joy, and becoming individuals we get to know, grow with, and love. Many of us weren't prepared for the possibility of losing a baby, so it felt like our world shattered when it happened.

In social psychology, there is something called the shattered assumptions theory that Ronnie Janoff-Bulman developed. It describes how traumatic events can have a shattering effect on our view of ourselves and the world. Suddenly we're faced with realizing our vulnerability, and now everything that felt safe and secure before seems uncertain.

For example, maybe you put your faith in religious beliefs, believing that a higher power always protects you. Then, a tragic loss brings everything into question: *Why would God allow something like this? This seems cruel, not the kind like I thought God to be. Is God even real?* As these questions linger, they often cause very real physical symptoms similar to post-traumatic stress disorder (PTSD), like increased heart rate, high blood pressure, and the release of stress hormones like cortisol.

How do we navigate this new and unexpected version of reality with strength and resilience when we feel fragile and unsettled? Even something as simple as figuring out what to do with the nursery, gifts, and other items we prepared for our little one can be a lot to contend with. In this chapter, we will explore these topics, discussing strategies for coming to terms with our loss, making necessary practical decisions, and shaping our narrative to regain a sense of control.

Coming to Terms

There comes a point when you must come to terms with your loss. Coming to terms means you accept what has happened and find ways to manage the loss's impact on you. It doesn't mean forgetting it or pretending it never happened. It means accepting the situation for what it is and allowing yourself to heal and move forward.

> *I'll never forget how surreal it felt when our family was gathered at the hospital, hoping and praying for the best. When the doctor told us that our sweet baby wouldn't make it, our hearts shattered into a million pieces.*
>
> *Day after day, I woke up wishing things were different, that it had all been a mistake, and she'd somehow be back with me. But as the days continued, I finally had to accept that that would never happen. Life had to go on, even though she wouldn't be in it.*
>
> *One thing that comforted me was the memory of the moment I learned I was pregnant with her. You hear people say it was the*

happiest moment of their lives, and for me, it was true. There are no words in any language that can describe the joy I felt. It was unlike anything I'd experienced before or since. Even though she died, the memory of learning I was pregnant with her is a gift that can never be taken away. In the pitch black of sadness, that's the one thing that brought me moments of light.

So, using the light of her memory to guide my way, I started taking small steps toward finding my new normal way of life: getting out of bed, making plans with friends, and giving myself the space to grieve when I needed to. It hasn't been an easy road, but it's leading me forward rather than keeping me stuck in a past that I can't change.

—Cameron, 37

Coming to terms with a loss doesn't happen overnight. It can be a process that takes weeks, months, or even years—and for good reason. Facing the loss opens us up to feel the full force of our emotions and thoughts surrounding it. It takes time and purposeful effort to sort through it all and respond in a way we can handle. There is no magic one-size-fits-all solution to get there. So we must try different things to find what works for us. Here are some simple solutions to get started.

<u>Express yourself</u>. A helpful step toward coming to terms can be to cry it out or talk things through with a friend. Expressing ourselves helps us process the complex emotions involved. Sometimes we simply have to say: "I lost my baby, and it SUCKS!" Just making that admission of our feelings and getting them out can be a big step toward acceptance.

Another helpful response is to <u>practice resilience</u>. Being resilient is about having determination, discipline, and a never-give-up attitude. Resilience behaves like a girdle for acceptance, encircling us as we fight emotional challenges and keeping us from falling apart. It helps us to be optimistic, understanding that this loss is a chapter, not the end of the book. At the same time, even with a resilient attitude, we may still experience periods of withdrawal and disbelief. These experiences are a natural part of the process of acceptance despite our resilience.

<u>Set positive intentions for yourself</u>. Affirmations are empowering statements individuals speak to themselves to foster self-belief and optimism. Speaking affirmations with meaningful words or phrases like "I will get through this" and "This will not break me" can be influential in setting positive intentions following a pregnancy or infant loss. This practice is about more than just positive thinking; it's a way to actively engage with your healing process. By verbalizing your affirmations, you acknowledge your pain and assert your strength and resilience. Making it a daily habit provides a means to shift your focus onto acceptance and recovery, which helps to build a mindset that propels you toward healing. You can go to www.rememberingcherubs.org/rc-affirmations to hear an original song of affirmation written and performed by *The Pregnancy Loss Guidebook* author Monica Sholar Anderson. It's a mantra of powerful affirmations you can listen to or repeat out loud.

<u>Do what works for you</u>. As we work toward acceptance, people around us can sometimes get in the way. Without intending to, their actions can hinder our progress and make things even more challenging. For example, some folks might expect us to "move on" or "get over it" within a certain timeframe, not understanding that acceptance and grief don't follow a neat little schedule.

Others might trigger our emotions with thoughtless comments or actions. And then there are those who may try to distract us from our grief altogether, urging us to stay busy or avoid talking about it. These well-meaning people in our lives can ultimately create more stress and anxiety as we try to make forward progress.

You have permission to block out any thoughts—or people—that take away from your well-being rather than add to it. It's okay to set boundaries and temporarily distance yourself while keeping your eyes on the prize—finding acceptance in a way that works best for you. In the end, you will be stronger for it.

<u>Take your time</u>. When faced with a traumatic loss, some people suppress the experience as a temporary defense mechanism. Suppressing the experience can be seen as a self-protective strategy that gives a person time to temporarily set aside the painful emotions until they are emotionally ready to confront them. Then they gradually process and come to terms with the reality of the situation. Though this approach can have its benefits, we wouldn't suggest suppression as a long-term solution to coming to terms with a loss.

<u>Talk to a professional</u>. Sometimes we can try our hardest, and it still feels like we are stuck in a rut with no progress toward acceptance. Consider talking with a counselor or therapist to break out of this cycle. Caring professionals can provide game-changing insight that might not come so easily to you on your own. Chapter 8 has great information on finding and building a good-fit relationship with a professional counselor or therapist.

Coming to terms with a loss may be no easy feat, but taking the time to process and express our emotions, adopt a resilient attitude, and be intentional with our efforts, gives us a good start at finding peace again.

What to Do with the Nursery, Gifts, and Other Items

Now that it's all said and done and reality is starting to set in, you may wonder what to do with the gifts and items you got for your baby and nursery. For some of us, it's hard to part with these items because they hold a special place in our hearts. Finding joy in them can be too painful, so they just sit in a corner and collect dust. But there are others who want to move on from the pain, and they get rid of everything on a whim. While discarding items may give us relief in the moment, it can lead to regret down the road, leaving us wishing we could have a pleasant reminder of our baby.

There is no right or wrong way to handle any stuff left behind. But we should take our time to make decisions we won't regret, really reflecting on what will bring us peace of mind in the long run. Fortunately, we have options to choose from. Let's explore some insight from parents who have been through similar experiences. Their perspective may help you decide on an option that feels right.

Option 1: Communicate your preferences even if you are undecided

> *By the time we got home from the hospital, my sister-in-law had cleared out every shred of all the baby stuff. I was stunned and felt violated. I know she was only trying to help, but it made things worse. It felt like now I had gone through two losses; the loss of my baby and all evidence that he ever existed. I wish I had been able to communicate that I hadn't yet decided what I wanted to do with all the items but that it was my decision to make—not anyone else's.*
>
> —Claire, 32

Even if you haven't decided what to do with your baby's things, make it known to the people around you that this is a personal decision and that when you are ready to take action, you will communicate your next steps and may even ask for their help. Sometimes well-meaning friends and family members get involved and remove things without consulting you first. While they may be trying to spare you pain, their actions can have the opposite effect. Be sure to express your preferences as soon as possible.

Option 2: Keep everything for a future pregnancy

> *After our loss, I held onto the baby clothes and things we had purchased. It wasn't something I had planned on doing—in*

> *fact, as I packed away our nursery, I fully intended on selling or donating everything.*
>
> *But as I held each onesie and tiny sock in my hands, something inside me shifted. These things represented so much more than just material possessions—they were symbols of hope for the future. So we kept them.*
>
> *Of course, this decision wasn't without its challenges. At times, just the very sight of them brought up painful memories and emotions. But when our rainbow baby finally arrived, it was all worth it. We dressed her in those same tiny clothes we had kept for so long, and it felt like everything had come full circle.*
>
> *We were just so glad we never gave up hope of adding to our family. Somehow hanging on to these things helped keep our hope alive.*
>
> —Brooklyn, 24

Some people keep clothes, toys, and other things to inspire hope that they will have another baby. It's a valid option that should be considered.

Option 3: Pack everything up and store it

> *My best friend offered to gather all the clothes and toys we had collected. She said she would keep them at her place until I was ready to decide what to do with them. I felt relieved knowing that I didn't have to make an immediate decision. It wasn't until a year later that I finally felt strong enough to deal with it. I ended up donating most of it but kept a few things for a memory box.*
>
> —Emma, 33

If it's too difficult for you to deal with items right away, have a friend or family member pack everything up in a safe place until you're emotionally prepared to decide what to do with them—or do it yourself if you feel up to it. Then, once you're in a better state of mind, you can decide what you want to do with the items permanently.

Option 4: Donate items to a local hospital

> *I felt a sense of accomplishment after donating some of my baby's belongings. Though my baby wasn't here, their life still served a purpose and mattered in the grand scheme of things. I felt comforted by that.*
>
> —Jasmine, 27

If you feel overwhelmed by having physical reminders of your loss around your home, consider donating the items to your local hospital. Hospitals often need supplies for their neonatal intensive care units (NICU). You can donate unused booties, blankets, and caps to a hospital's NICU or bereavement program. A number of national organizations also accept donations of baby items. An Internet search will turn up lots of options to choose from.

Option 5: Sell or consign the items

> *My aunt got a table at a Mom 2 Mom sale and was able to sell every single thing. She got a nice amount of money and used it to treat me. She'd randomly send lunch to my job or order me flowers. Just little things to make me feel cared for, and I really appreciated that. I wouldn't have done that for myself, but I was so grateful she did.*
>
> —Hazel, 30

You could sell or consign your items if you don't want to donate them. Several online platforms let you sell or consign new or used baby items, such as eBay, Craigslist, and Reloveable. Take the profits to do something nice for yourself or donate to a charity.

Option 6: Give the items to a friend or family member

> *A lady down the street from me learned she was pregnant just a month after I did. A few months after my loss, I put together a gift basket filled with clothes, toys, and even gift cards. It was an indescribable feeling to see that baby a year later wearing some of the clothes. I'd be lying if I said I didn't prefer to see my own baby wearing them. But since that wasn't possible, seeing them put to good use felt good.*
>
> —Amina, 35

You may consider giving friends or family members who are expecting a baby your unused items to pass on something special.

Option 7: Keep things for memory-making

> *In the end, I decided to keep all my daughter's belongings. I thought it was a nice way to honor her short life while also allowing me some closure. It wasn't easy gathering everything up, but I got through it. My collection includes everything from sonogram pictures and hospital bracelets to tiny clothing and blankets she never got to wear or use. These items are my only connection to her. Although they are tucked away in boxes now, I can pull them out whenever I want, which brings me comfort.*
>
> —Ariana, 26

You can save things that were meant for or used by your baby. Put them in a special container or memory box as a lasting reminder of the love held for your little one.

Deciding what to do with gifts given to you for your baby can be tricky. This can be especially true for gifts that are handmade or personalized. The sentimental value can make them hard to part with and, at the same time, can make them hard to keep.

The best advice is to honor the way you feel above all else. If keeping a gift feels too overwhelming, don't keep it. You can offer to return it to the giver or part with it in any of the ways listed above.

On the other hand, if someone requests their gift back before you're emotionally prepared to decide your plans for it, it's okay to take your time coming to a decision. If you feel uncomfortable having this conversation, get a family member or friend to help communicate on your behalf while you focus on your well-being.

Some people store away unopened gifts until they are more emotionally ready to process them. Taking time to focus on yourself and circling back when you're in a better position to make a decision is a wise choice and a great way to demonstrate self-care when you need it most.

The timing of some losses can mean that thank-you notes for baby shower gifts haven't even been sent yet. In these cases, sending an appreciation note isn't necessary. However, it can allow you to communicate the news of the loss while still showing appreciation for the gift. Consider writing that you will repurpose the item in a meaningful way, donate it to someone in need, or keep it in anticipation of another pregnancy in the future. And add that the item can be returned to them if requested.

Example:

> *Dear [Name],*
>
> *Thank you so much for your thoughtful and generous gift for our baby shower. We know that it came from a place of love.*
>
> *Unfortunately, due to a pregnancy loss, we will be unable to use this gift ourselves. We are deeply saddened by this loss, but we find comfort in*

knowing that with your gift, we can help another family in need. And so we will be gifting the item to an organization of our choice. We are so thankful that from our difficult situation, someone else will get this much-needed item for their journey into parenthood.

Words cannot express how grateful we are to you for your support, and we will continue to rely on it in the days ahead.

With much appreciation,

[Your Name]

Chapter 7 has additional guidance on how to tell people about your loss and how to deal with their reaction.

When deciding what to do with a nursery after losing a baby, the most important thing you can do is give yourself time and space to figure it out. If leaving the room as-is brings comfort, then, by all means, do it. But if it overwhelms you, allow yourself to make slow, gentle changes. You could pack up the nursery, knowing you don't have to make a permanent decision right away. Talking with a peer or a counselor can help you work through any conflicting feelings.

Another option is to repurpose the nursery room. Changing the nursery into a space for self-care can have great benefits.

After my miscarriage, my stomach tensed in knots every time I walked by the room that would have been my baby's. It was torture because it reminded me that my baby would never be there. I felt so powerless against that feeling. Around the same time, I had just started learning about breathing techniques to help with stress management. I needed a quiet place to try it, and that room was the only one in the house that would work.

One night before bed, I went in there and just sat on the floor for a while. Then I pulled out my phone and watched videos of the breathing techniques I was learning. Then I sat some more. I cried. I screamed. Then I went to bed. Let me tell you; it was one of the best night's sleep I'd had in a really long time. The next night I did the same thing. Before long, I started doing daily stretching there and yoga. Then slowly, throughout the months, I transformed the space into a sanctuary where I cared for myself.

I eventually put in a small desk and started doing my work there; it's actually where I started my nonprofit, Remembering Cherubs. The room was intended to be a space of love for my baby, and now I was channeling all that love toward myself and all the parents of loss I knew I wanted to help through my work.

Today, that room is my permanent workspace/workout room/ meditative space. I have the word LOVE in big, bold letters and words of affirmation on the wall. I also have it decorated with houseplants and greenery that makes me feel good. It's no longer a source of stress for me. Now it's a source of restoration and healing.

—Monica, 41

When transforming a nursery for yourself, focus on creating a sense of serenity. You can do this by decorating with pictures or artwork with personal significance—anything that makes you feel refreshed and recharged.

If you don't have an entire room, you can repurpose a corner or area with comfortable blankets, mats, or a chair. You don't have to make any grand gestures to make this space your own. Simply being there and doing things that build you up is enough.

In the grand scheme of things, it's alright if you don't know what to do with baby stuff left behind. Taking the time to think through your options or put off making a final decision until you are ready will help you choose what you feel most comfortable with. And creating a dedicated area for self-care can give you the space needed to come to terms with these new life changes.

Shaping your narrative

When we're in the new territory of moving on with life after a pregnancy or infant loss, it can feel like the world has broken. All the life adventures we had planned were suddenly canceled. The direction we thought we were headed has now spun a different way. We scramble to find order when it seems everything is topsy-turvy. But if you look at it from an objective point of view, you'll see that the world is still turning. And by searching for meaning among its broken parts, you can shape and rebuild your world in a way that makes you stronger than ever.

There is something called post-traumatic growth (PTG), which refers to positive psychological changes that individuals may experience after going through a traumatic event, such as pregnancy or infant loss. Despite the profound grief and pain associated with these losses, research suggests that some individuals can find ways to grow and develop in the aftermath. Post-traumatic growth doesn't negate or diminish the pain of the loss. Rather, it represents a parallel process of finding positive meaning and growth within the aftermath of trauma.

You may have heard the saying, "Find the positive in your situation." You do this by reflecting on the days since your loss happened and asking yourself probing questions: "What can I learn from this experience?" "How can I demonstrate resilience?" "What's inside me that's helping me get through it?"

The answers to your questions can reveal hidden strengths and perspectives that perhaps you hadn't considered. Maybe losing something treasured has taught you that life is precious, inspiring you to live more fully. Maybe you see this loss as a way to build a comeback story you write about in a book to help other people. Or maybe you recognize your grandmother's fighter spirit within you, a person who faced down challenges and always came out on top. By shaping your perspective of your experience, you are creating a narrative that evolves your story from one of loss to one of triumph over misfortune.

Take Talia's story, for example:

I've always been somewhat of a perfectionist, wanting everything to go exactly as planned. So when I had a miscarriage, followed by another one a year later, it really threw me for a loop. Every time I looked in the mirror, I saw a reminder of what could have been. The fact that I seemingly couldn't carry a baby to full term made me feel like a complete failure.

I felt envious of my friends who could easily conceive and carry a baby to term. It was hard to be around them without feeling a twinge of resentment. Why was it so easy for them and not me? What was wrong with me?

Through friends, I met a woman who had been through similar struggles as me. She had two living children and told me about the countless times she'd had miscarriages and how she used to blame herself too. She helped me educate myself and learn about all the incredible things my body did to protect me and the baby during my pregnancy.

I had to understand that some things are simply outside our control, no matter how perfect we may want them to be. Learning all this information and hearing her story made me realize that my body was doing the best it could—it certainly wasn't trying to work against me. This body had gotten me through a lot. So, I shouldn't hold a grudge against it.

From then on, I made a promise to myself to be kinder to myself and my body. The more I blamed myself, the harder it would be to heal and move on with my life. Now, I choose to focus on loving myself despite my story not being a perfect one. I deserve it.

—Talia, 29

Our losses don't have to define or limit who we are. We don't have to brand ourselves as a "parent of loss." Instead, through our actions and resilience, we get to take ownership of our self-view, spinning it in a more positive light. We get to be champions after loss, survivors who faced the darkest night and outlasted it. We get to be unbreakable, even though we may bend. We get to be parents of children, who, despite it all, were loved, and whose memory we will cherish. That's a narrative worth striving for.

Conclusion

Losing a pregnancy or infant forces us to adjust to a new reality. We may be unsure what to do with the items we have collected and lovingly prepared for our little ones. But whether we decide to part with some things or keep others, we should remember that taking the time to make our decision is always the best option. As we come to terms with our loss, we can shape our narrative in a way that helps us accept those things we can't change and take control of what we can.

Rest Stop

1. **Take a moment to reflect**. Write down a lesson from this chapter that will help guide your way, like speaking positively with affirmations. Visit www.rememberingcherubs.org/rc-affirmations to hear words of affirmation set to music.

2. **Shape your narrative.** Studies show that writing about events in our lives can help us understand them and respond to them in ways that benefit us. Try writing out your story. Reflect on your experience and ask yourself questions that will help you realize your strengths and manage the impact of your loss in beneficial ways.

3. **Take the *Crawl. Walk. Run. Soar.* self-assessment:**

    How are you feeling today? (circle one)

    Crawling – Making small but determined actions on your path to healing.

    Walking – Building momentum and making steady, consistent progress.

    Running – Taking rapid strides despite challenges.

Soaring – Reaching new heights as you move forward toward an optimistic future.

Remember: One day, you may soar, and the next, you may crawl. And that's okay. Healing isn't a linear journey with a set destination. It is continual progress toward feeling better.

4. **Take a Break**. Give your mind a well-deserved break, then come back fresh and ready to dive into the next chapter tomorrow.

Notes

Part Two
Finding Resilience

Chapter 5
Coping Well

Grief can manifest in many ways, from feeling sad and angry to feeling numb and disconnected from others. It's common to have a range of emotions and grief reactions after a pregnancy or infant loss. In this chapter, we will dive deep into understanding grief and the four main types of grief reactions: emotional, physical, cognitive, and behavioral. We'll also explore different skills, strategies, and actions that will help us cope with it in healthy and healing ways.

Understanding Grief

Grief is a person's emotional response to the experience of loss. It can look different for everyone and vary in intensity and duration. There are sporadic highs and lows—some days, we might feel sad, but other days, things may feel more bearable. Grieving is difficult, but we can make it through by doing things that help us feel stronger and supported.

People often underestimate the grief associated with miscarriage. There's an unfortunate misconception that parents who lose their baby early in pregnancy don't feel as much grief. However, most researchers haven't been able to support this idea. The grief can be the same whether you lose your baby at five or twenty-five weeks. Grief is determined by how it affects someone emotionally, not by the duration of the experience that triggered it. According to research, up to 50 percent of miscarrying women and 48 percent of their partners may experience psychological distress in the weeks and months following the loss, including anxiety, depression, and even PTSD. But with time, care, and treatment (if needed), grief and depressive symptoms often reduce—the same is true for other forms of pregnancy loss.

Grief from pregnancy and infant loss impacts individuals in all communities. However, these effects are often magnified in marginalized groups due to factors such as race, socioeconomic status, sexual orientation, and religious background. For example:

- Race – In Chapter 2, we mentioned that Black women experience pregnancy and infant loss disproportionately more than White women and women of other races. Studies have shown the loss rates are at least twice as high as any other racial or ethnic group (Van & Meleis, 2002). The significance of these losses may be downplayed by family, friends, and health professionals because they occur so often. Normalizing such an emotionally significant event can severely impact the grieving process of these mothers.

- Culture and Religion – Cultural and religious beliefs can significantly influence how parents experience and cope with grief (Allahdadian & Irajpour, 2015). In some cultures or religions, there may be stigma or silence surrounding pregnancy loss. Some belief systems even attribute pregnancy loss to divine will or personal wrongdoing, which can lead to self-blame or spiritual distress that impacts parents' relationship with their religious community.

- Socioeconomic Status – Parents from lower socioeconomic backgrounds may experience intensified grief following loss due to financial stressors that compound the emotional impact of the loss. They might also have fewer resources to seek professional mental health services to cope with their loss, which could lead to prolonged and unaddressed grief (Gipson et al., 2008).

- Sexual Orientation – Parents in the LGBTQIA+ community face unique challenges from prejudice, discrimination, and lack of culturally competent care, which can add complexity to their grief experiences (Lacombe-Duncan et al., 2022).

Receiving support and resources that are sensitive to these marginalized groups is a must to ensure their experiences and grief are validated.

Most people understand grief in the context of losing a loved one. But we can also experience it over other situations, like losing a job, divorce, or facing an illness. Understandably, the grief from pregnancy or infant loss may bring up grief from these other situations, which can complicate and compound an already fragile experience. Being aware of coping strategies, which we will cover later in this chapter, can help us manage our reactions.

Grief versus depression: which am I feeling? Grief and depression, while often confused with one another, are different. Grief is the emotional reaction to loss; it's a natural process that needs to be allowed and felt but doesn't always need professional support. Depression, however, is a formal mental health diagnosis (a mood disorder) that can last for weeks, months, or even longer. When left untreated, symptoms of depression may linger or even worsen without the help of a mental health professional—or sometimes medication. Thankfully, tons of research has been done on grief and depression; when properly treated, we can see great success in managing both.

There are different kinds of grief to consider.

Bereavement and Mourning

Bereavement and mourning are terms often used interchangeably but have different meanings. Bereavement is the period when people work through their grief. On the other hand, mourning is the outward expression of grief. It's a visible and public display of grief that encompasses the rituals, behaviors, and customs that individuals engage in to honor and cope with their loss, such as attending funerals or memorial services, writing letters in remembrance, and visiting gravesites. Think of it this way: while bereavement is an internal experience centered on how you feel, mourning is how it manifests externally, centered on what you do.

Complicated Grief

Complicated grief, also known as prolonged grief disorder (PGD), is when the grieving process becomes prolonged and intense. It makes it difficult for parents to adjust to their loss and resume daily activities. Unlike normal grief, which tends to fade over time, complicated grief persists or worsens over an extended period. It's a recognized mental health condition that may require professional intervention. Common symptoms include intense longing for the deceased, persistent emotional pain, and difficulty accepting the loss. Complicated grief can also manifest as bitterness, anger, guilt, or a sense of meaninglessness. According to the *Diagnostic and Statistical Manual of Mental Disorders (DSM-5)*, the diagnosis of complicated grief requires experiencing symptoms for at least six months after the loss. However, anyone experiencing these symptoms should seek professional support sooner rather than later.

Disenfranchised Grief

According to Dr. Kenneth J. Doka, people experience disenfranchised grief when they grieve a loss that is not or cannot be openly acknowledged, publicly mourned, or socially supported. The grief of miscarriage, stillbirth, infant loss, and loss due to termination for maternal health or fetal anomaly are perfect examples of disenfranchised grief. These forms of loss are often stigmatized and glossed over by society. As a result, many parents who experience disenfranchised grief feel alone and misunderstood, without much emotional support. They are trying to process their loss in an environment where it isn't recognized, and people don't accept or value what they are going through.

For example, when parents in the LGBTQIA+ community experience a pregnancy loss, they may encounter disenfranchised grief due to societal and cultural attitudes toward their unique situation. Imagine a same-sex couple who had been trying to conceive through assisted reproductive technologies. After multiple attempts and significant emotional investment, they finally achieve a successful pregnancy. However, tragically, they experience a miscarriage. Despite their profound loss, they may face dismissive responses from others who fail to recognize the depth of their grief. Some individuals might not acknowledge their parental status or the significance of their loss because they don't feel the couple conforms to traditional notions of family. This lack of validation and understanding can intensify the couple's feelings of isolation and add an additional layer of complexity to their grieving process, leading to disenfranchised grief.

Incongruent Grief

Incongruent grief is when parents experience and express grief differently. It refers to the intensity of their grief and how they process it. One parent may be more outwardly emotional and expressive, while the other may be more stoic and internalize their grief. One parent may use defense mechanisms like denial or avoidance while the other engages with the loss head-on. The length of time spent in mourning can also vary significantly between parents; one might struggle with emotions months after the loss, while the other feels ready to move on much sooner. Chapter 6 has detailed insight into the ways partners can cope with incongruent grief.

Mourning and bereavement are the most recognized forms of grief, while society often overlooks complicated, disenfranchised, and incongruent grief. By understanding the different types of grief we are experiencing, we can learn more about the ways to manage them effectively. The following two sections will show us how to do that.

Grief Reactions

Grief is a universal emotion that everyone experiences at some point in their lives. People react to it differently, usually in four ways: emotionally, physically, cognitively, and behaviorally. Let's explore what each grief reaction entails.

Emotional Reactions

Sadness is often the first emotion we feel, but this can give way to other feelings like anxiety, bitterness, guilt, helplessness, and despair.

- People may also experience intense sensations of loneliness, yearning for what was lost, or feeling like they are not in control of their lives.
- We may also have mood swings or even feel numb to any emotions.

Every holiday was a difficult and emotional experience for me. On Mother's Day, I felt the absence of my baby. Christmas was even harder. But nothing compared to the anniversary of my baby's death. Every year it was like ripping open an old wound just when it was starting to heal.

But what was strange to me was how losing my baby triggered grief over the loss of my mother, which had happened years before. It felt like these two losses were connected in some way. On the anniversary of my mother's death, I found myself grieving her and my baby. This was incredibly painful and confusing and seemed almost implausible that grief for one could bring up such intense grief for the other.

—Bianca, 34

Grief is not always isolated to one singular event; it can stir up emotions tied to past experiences of loss. The intensity of Bianca's grief over her pregnancy loss brought to the surface unresolved feelings about the loss of her parent. The common thread of loss caused these different instances of grief to intertwine, amplifying her overall emotional response.

Regardless of our emotional reactions, we should remember that our feelings are valid and deserve care.

Physical Reactions

- Having physical reactions like headaches, body pains, skin rashes, and changes in appetite can all be signs of being overwhelmed by grief.
- High blood pressure, sleep disturbances, lack of energy, and indigestion can all signal that your body is having difficulty dealing with the stress you may be going through.
- People may also feel tightness in their chest or throat and shortness of breath.

If we don't recognize these signs and take steps to reduce our stress, it can negatively impact our health and well-being. Chapter 10 highlights self-care practices that can support our efforts.

Cognitive Reactions (reactions related to thinking and reasoning)

- Grief can manifest itself cognitively in many ways, such as short-term memory loss, difficulty concentrating, and confusion. Some people experience forgetfulness or find it hard to make even simple decisions in the face of their loss.
- Individuals may also feel lost and struggle to make sense of the circumstances, which can lead to an increase or decrease in dreams or even nightmares.

- People sometimes disbelieve that the loss happened, preoccupying themselves with obsessive thoughts about their baby. In some cases, there have even been reports of hallucinations where people have seen and heard their deceased child.

My pregnancy had gone smoothly, and my little boy seemed incredibly healthy; I thought it would be a smooth ride from there. But then he was born prematurely, and despite the doctors' best efforts, he died shortly after. The days that followed were a blur, but one thing I'll never forget is the random images that would come to me. I'd be going about my day and suddenly see his face and the moment the nurses had placed his body in my arms. There was a small tear on his neck because his skin wasn't fully developed and had split during birth. Reliving those random moments felt like having nightmares while awake.

—Angela, 24

Angela's cognitive reaction came in the form of intrusive thoughts, seeing mental images, and reliving the details of her loss.

Reactions like these are normal, but we shouldn't ignore them. They can be a sign that we need to take time for ourselves or seek help.

Behavioral Reactions

- Behavioral reactions can show up in different ways. People might eat too much or too little, avoid things that remind them of the baby, cry, blame others, or use alcohol or drugs.

- Grief isn't about just feeling sad. It can also mean doing less and not caring for yourself, like brushing your teeth, eating healthy food, or exercising.

- Behavioral reactions can also present as an overall lack of interest in activities that used to bring joy, such as work, socializing, world events, and sex.

It's important to recognize that these reactions are a natural and common part of dealing with grief.

Grief can be a complicated, winding journey. Some days will be better than others. In the next section, we'll look at coping techniques that help us not just get through the day but conquer it.

Coping Skills, Strategies, and Actions

Now that we better understand grief and its reactions, it's time to confront how we'll cope with it. Coping means adapting to the new conditions in our life and finding ways to overcome the challenges.

Coping skills refer to the methods and behaviors you rely on to get you through difficult situations.

For example, when faced with a challenge, do you confront it head-on or retreat from it? Do you have a mindset of overcoming obstacles, or do you feel defeated by them? Do you see yourself as a victim or champion when telling your story? Your answers can help you gain insight into your natural coping behaviors. If you naturally show strength in the face of adversity, you're off to a great start in your ability to cope well. But if your tendencies are more passive, don't worry; it just means you have room to develop your coping skills. We'll look at some strategies that can help.

Coping strategies are different from coping skills. A coping strategy is a plan you make to cope with your situation. Two common coping strategies are emotion-focused coping and problem-focused coping.

Emotion-focused coping is when we make a plan to manage our emotions. After something bad happens, we can only control how we respond to it. Emotion-focused coping helps us focus on what we can do instead of what we cannot change.

> *I lost my infant daughter to sudden infant death syndrome. I was shocked. Sad. Angry. And grief had me in a chokehold. I knew I had to find ways to cope with the pain because I was starting to lash out at other people in frustration.*
>
> *Society taught me that leaning into my emotions wasn't the manly thing to do. But I knew that bottling them up and not expressing them in healthy ways wasn't a smart thing to do. So I decided that for the first time in my life, I would allow myself to feel my emotions, not stuff them down like I usually would.*
>
> *Sometimes all I did was cry—in the shower, in the car, or masking it behind sweat at the gym. I wasn't using words, but my tears felt like self-expression. Even still, crying wasn't enough to get me to a better place.*
>
> *My wife had been journaling about her thoughts and feelings, and I could see how impactful that was for her. I tried to mimic what she was doing, but writing just wasn't my thing. The words get lost in translation from my brain to the pen. What I was able to do was put how I was feeling on a sticky note—just a word or two. For example, I would write, "I'm pissed." Then I would look at the note and explore why I felt pissed. I realized it was because so much had been taken from me in my life from years of bouncing in and out of foster care when I was a kid; my daughter was another precious thing that was taken against my will. So I was angry about it. Nothing I could do would bring her back.*

Once I understood why I felt how I felt, I had to come up with a way to deal with it instead of allowing the feelings to consume me. Instead of focusing on the obvious—that she wasn't coming back—I tried to reframe it and say, yes, my daughter isn't here anymore, but I got to have her for the short time I did. She brought me joy and love, and I have my memories; those gifts will never be taken away. So I let my mind focus more on the good of the situation rather than all the bad I couldn't change.

Those little sticky notes saved me. Word-by-word and emotion-by-emotion, they helped me process and cope with the greatest loss of my life.

—Mike, 38

Mike had a plan: *figure out why I feel how I feel, then do what I can to feel better*. Focusing on what he could change, rather than what he couldn't, was a solid emotion-focused coping strategy that led to life-changing results.

Problem-focused coping is a strategy that helps us deal with difficult situations by directing our energy toward finding a solution. It helps us identify the things that we can control and take steps to address them.

I never imagined my beautiful baby would be taken away from me so soon. He was born prematurely and only lived for a few days. The loss was a heavy blow, and despite people around me saying, "Give it time; time heals all wounds," the pain still wasn't going away.

One of the biggest problems for me was that every day looked different. A different thing would trigger me; whether seeing a baby on a TV commercial or looking at all the baby stuff we had collected, something would send me into an emotional tailspin.

I felt I had no control over my grief reactions because I was constantly triggered.

I went to a bereavement group put on through my hospital, which helped a lot. A woman in the group told me to "plan what you can." It was a phrase she created to help her get through the days. The idea is that you map out a daily plan to leave the room to feel what you feel and figure out the best way to deal with it.

For example, I'm a morning person and feel more productive at that time. So she suggested that every morning at the same time, I get quiet and allow my mind to process everything I was feeling, reflecting on the triggers that set me off the day before and figuring out a solution to combat it.

I gave it a try. A big trigger for me was the smell of this major brand of soap. It was a brand I often used at home, and the hospital had also included a sample bar in the care kit they gave me. I remember the smell of the soap wafting up next to me in the neonatal intensive care unit as my baby fought for his life. Ever since then, every time I smelled it, it reminded me of being in that room, which reminded me of my baby's death. The scent of the soap was a trigger. Once I realized that, I removed all the products in our house that smelled like it. I was glad to have one less trigger to deal with.

It's only been a few months, but I still stick to my "plan what you can" sessions, sometimes even more than once a day. It's like that quiet time allows me to solve little problems that pop up, and I get the mental space to work out a solution that helps me over the hurdle. My child's death still feels like a big open wound, but using problem-focused coping strategies has made it easier for me to find peace.

—Akila, 33

Through her "plan what you can" sessions, Akila identified her problem: the scent trigger. Then she eliminated the scent to avoid getting triggered by it over and over again. Removing the trigger was a great solution and a perfect problem-focused coping strategy.

Problem-focused coping empowers us to take action and regain a sense of control amidst our grief, while emotion-focused coping allows for the necessary emotional release. Rather than relying solely on one approach or the other, embracing both strategies can stimulate our resilience and support our healing.

Now that we have learned two powerful coping strategies, let's look at some simple actions we can take to cope well.

Psychology often talks about coping in two ways: healthy and unhealthy. Healthy actions can have long-term positive effects on our ability to cope well. Some examples are:

- Regular exercise to reduce stress
- Eating well to support energy levels
- Mindfulness practices to find balance
- Relaxation to release tension
- Self-expression to avoid pent-up emotions
- Self-affirmation to gain confidence
- Social support to feel less alone

Unhealthy actions, on the other hand, give us temporary relief and make us feel good in the moment but can have long-term negative consequences. Some examples are:

- Smoking cigarettes or using other tobacco products, such as cigars and pipes
- Self-medicating with alcohol or drugs

- Overeating or undereating
- Withdrawing from friends and family
- Engaging in dangerous activities like reckless driving
- Overspending money on unnecessary items
- Excessive gaming or watching television for hours at a time without interacting with others

We should be on the lookout for when we start relying too heavily on unhealthy actions that don't really help us process or heal the underlying pain, like the excessive gaming or frequent binge-watching TV as mentioned above.

Don't get us wrong; a marathon of *The Golden Girls* reruns and some emotional support brownies can be just the thing that helps you get through the day. But if it becomes your go-to day after day, you have to realize that it's just a temporary fix that isn't helping you in the long run.

Remember: A coping strategy is a plan to cope with your situation. Coping skills are your behaviors and actions to carry out the plan. This one-two punch is the secret weapon to coping well with loss.

Conclusion

In this chapter, we've discussed the different kinds of grief, plus grief reactions, and the skills, strategies, and actions necessary to cope with it. The truth is, losing a baby is never easy, and the grief that follows looks different for everyone. But with the right mindset and the coping techniques available to us, we can come out stronger and more resilient than ever.

Rest Stop

1. **Take a moment to reflect**. Write down a few coping strategies you can follow when feeling overwhelmed with grief, and put them in a place where they are easy to see, like on your phone or by the mirror. This way, you can access helpful tools no matter where you are.

2. **Take the *Crawl. Walk. Run. Soar.* self-assessment:**

    How are you feeling today? (circle one)

    Crawling – Making small but determined actions on your path to healing.

    Walking – Building momentum and making steady, consistent progress.

    Running – Taking rapid strides despite challenges.

    Soaring – Reaching new heights as you move forward toward an optimistic future.

    Remember: One day, you may soar, and the next, you may crawl. And that's okay. Healing isn't a linear journey with a set destination. It is continual progress toward feeling better.

3. **Take a break**. Give your mind a well-deserved break, then come back fresh and ready to dive into the next chapter tomorrow.

Notes

Chapter 6
The Partner-Parent Perspective: Being Support*ed* and Being Support*ive*

I wish we had both been able to grieve together and receive support in the aftermath of the loss instead of feeling like only one of us mattered.

—Harper, 33

Although pregnancy and infant loss can be distressing for any individual, the impact on the partner is often overlooked. While everyone tends to focus on the person who physically went through the experience, it's important to know that both people may be reeling emotionally.

Unfortunately, society tends to tell partners that they have to be strong, that they need to help the other person through this difficult time—but what about them? What about their own emotional needs? Their grief often goes unrecognized or minimized because they didn't physically have the loss.

Cultural norms surrounding men, particularly, and their masculinity during grief, can create added challenges. Masculinity is often a double-edged sword. On the one hand, people can view it as empowering—yet when grief hits home, men can be expected to bury their feelings and suffer in silence instead of being allowed to express themselves openly or reach out for help.

Being a partner-parent after a loss has a unique set of challenges, no matter their gender. This chapter will offer guidance to ease some of their strain. It will cover how to get support, cope with incongruent grief, and ten ways in which they can be supportive partners. You may not have a partner-parent situation, but read this chapter anyway; there is still valuable information you can learn from.

Supporting the Supporter—*Taking Care of Yourself*

Supporting our partner is necessary. However, taking care of ourselves first can help us accomplish that. "Secure your own mask before helping others" isn't just advice for the airplane; ensuring we're okay gives us more strength and stability to provide meaningful love and support.

You might feel selfish for having needs of your own. But don't. Consider that if a car ran without ever stopping for fuel or an oil change, its engine would eventually give out. No one expects something like this from their vehicle, so don't put those unreasonable expectations on yourself. Give yourself permission to take care of your own needs.

Have you ever heard of "self-care" but wondered what it really means? It refers to making time for activities that help keep your well-being on track—just like the car that needs regular maintenance to run smoothly. If guilty feelings or other challenges keep getting in the way of prioritizing yourself, here are some ways to overcome them and practice proper self-care:

Recognize that self-care isn't selfish: Taking care of ourselves isn't selfish; it's essential. We shouldn't view it as a luxury or an indulgence. The idea that we must give our all to support our partner is a great sentiment, but if we don't also prioritize our own well-being, it won't last. We must allow ourselves those restorative moments without feeling like we're doing something wrong. Focusing on self-care first doesn't just benefit us, our partner will also benefit from a stronger support system.

The days had been incredibly difficult for my spouse and me. We were grieving the sudden loss of her pregnancy at twenty-eight weeks, and it felt like we were spinning out of control. I had been trying to care for both of us but could barely keep myself together. This would have been my first child and her second.

I needed some time away, so I took a drive along the lakeshore. After a half hour on the road, I stopped at a fishing spot overlooking a lake. Being there brought up a memory of me fishing with my dad. We were out on the ice when it broke open, and we both fell in. I screamed to my dad for help before my head completely submerged. I could feel the struggle beneath the water from him trying to get to me. But he couldn't because his leg had gotten tangled in something in the water. As an adult, I can't imagine the terror he must have felt. He wanted to save me even before saving himself, but he couldn't do anything until he freed himself. Eventually, he managed to get untangled with help from nearby people who hoisted us both out of the water.

As I stood there, thinking about that memory, it dawned on me that I was in a similar position as my father had been. My wife and I were both drowning, but I couldn't support her without first tending to my own needs. This was the first time I truly understood the concept of self-care—right there, thinking back on that memory sealed it for me. If I didn't take care of myself, I wouldn't be able to care for anyone else. It was such a simple notion, but now I understood it more than ever.

Sometimes when I go on my lakeshore drives to decompress, I still get a nagging feeling that I'm neglecting my duties toward my spouse. But then I think about that lake incident and remember that I'm doing exactly what I'm supposed to be doing.

—Miguel, 31

Start small: If the idea of taking time for yourself feels overwhelming, start with small steps, like taking a ten-minute walk to clear your head. You can do this on your lunch break, before bed, or even right when you wake up. These little moments can add up over time and help you build self-care habits.

Set boundaries: Setting boundaries when your partner needs support can be challenging. But you have to recognize your own mental and emotional limits first. Communicate compassionately and discuss what you can do in that moment rather than what you can't. This will allow both of you to move at a manageable pace while respecting each other's needs. It takes practice, but establishing these boundaries will serve both of you in the long run.

My wife had an ectopic pregnancy, and she was struggling emotionally. She was fixated on all the plans she would never fulfill with our baby. I was doing my best to be there for her—I listened, held her hand, and tried to encourage her through it. But no matter how hard I tried, it felt like nothing ever seemed to be enough.

As someone who works from home, my wife regularly came into my office and had emotional outbursts. While I understood what she was going through, it was starting to interfere with my work and take up every minute of my time. It wasn't just impacting my work life but also affecting me on a deeper level. I love her, so seeing her go through such emotional turmoil was gut-wrenching. If I could have taken away her pain so she wouldn't have had to go through it, I would have in a heartbeat. But that wasn't an option. Every day felt like an overwhelming struggle as I put aside my needs to prioritize hers.

After a particularly rough night with several emotional episodes from my wife, I knew something had to change — I was becoming worn out. The next day, I sat down with her and opened up about how I had been feeling. I told her that I needed to set some boundaries because I was starting to feel like I was being pulled under.

Unfortunately, the conversation didn't go as well as I had hoped. She felt like I was saying she was a burden to me, which wasn't what I meant at all. As compassionately as possible, I explained that while it wasn't reasonable for her to walk into my office at any time without regard for what I was doing, we could instead schedule breaks where she and I could spend time together doing whatever she wanted or needed.

After a few days of setting and upholding these boundaries, my wife finally understood where I was coming from. Demonstrating my needs instead of just telling her about them helped us both. While some days were still difficult, giving each other space when needed without feeling guilty or obligated was a relief.

My wife appreciated these new boundaries too, because she realized that as much as she needed to grieve with me, she also needed the space to grieve on her own—something she hadn't allowed herself to do before. Knowing that we both understand the importance of boundaries has helped us weather this storm, and I'm confident it will continue to benefit us.

—Terry, 42

Seek out support: Having someone in your corner can be a game-changer when dealing with guilt over prioritizing your needs. Talking to a therapist, joining a support group, or even relying on the comfort of close friends and family members can make all the difference in acknowledging your needs. That extra level of emotional security will go a long way toward dispelling any nagging doubts that might prevent you from looking after yourself.

Practice self-compassion: Self-compassion means recognizing and accepting your limitations with grace. Being kind and understanding toward yourself can help you realize that you are doing the best you can. This is a powerful lesson you can carry forward.

Our baby was stillborn, and because of some severe complications from bleeding that threatened my wife's life, the doctors performed an emergency hysterectomy. This was crushing, to say the least. I sat by my wife's bedside day by day, trying to find the right words to comfort her, but I kept coming up empty. I felt overwhelmed by emotions—sadness, anger, and also guilt for some reason that I can't really explain. There were no easy answers and no perfect solutions to move forward. All I could offer was love and support through what would be a long journey of healing.

Talking with my mother-in-law reminded me that despite the grief and sadness surrounding us, we were doing our best with what we had. We were surviving each day, and that was enough. I didn't need to "fix" this, which I had a tendency to try to do in situations. Just getting through it was an accomplishment. Her daily reminders offered me the grace I needed and helped me not be hard on myself for not being able to do more.

—Tanner, 32

Now that we know how to support ourselves, the next section will help us understand how to get additional support if needed.

Understanding Your Support Needs

Trying to understand your support needs can be a trip, but it's a trip worth taking. It starts with self-reflection and asking yourself questions to better understand your needs, such as: What activities could make me feel better and help reduce stress? Is there something someone can do that would help me get through the day? Answering these questions will help you identify what support you need and how others can help.

There are five different ways people might show their support. Here are some habits you may recognize:

The Comforter: They are typically nurturing and comforting, and they make an effort to make you feel better with physical touch and words of encouragement or by simply being present by your side. They are usually good at listening and offering advice.

The Problem-Solver: They are logical and analytical and want to help you by finding a solution to your problem.

The Cheerleader: They are positive and upbeat and want to help you by providing motivation and encouragement. Cheerleaders try to help you see the silver lining in every situation.

The Listener: They are patient and attentive and want to help you by simply listening to you without judgment.

The Rock: They are reliable, supportive, and stable. Rocks are typically good at being there for others and are willing to take whatever action necessary to help you through what you're going through. They tend to be a good mix of being a comforter, problem-solver, cheerleader, and listener.

As we cope with our loss, sometimes we need a cheerleader, and other times just someone to listen. A balance of different supporters in your corner can help ensure you receive the full support you deserve.

That said, having support won't amount to a hill of beans if we don't communicate our needs. How will people know what to do if we don't tell them? Something as simple as "I could really use a beer and some time on the basketball court," can let your supporters know how they can show up for you in a way you will appreciate and benefit the most.

If you find yourself without any outside support to depend on, there are other options available for you. One is joining a support group for partners who have experienced loss. You can find groups in your area or online through an Internet search. Chapter 8 has additional ideas you can try. But nothing beats self-care. If you can't depend on anyone else, make sure you can rely on yourself.

Coping with Incongruent Grief

Incongruent grieving, as mentioned in the previous chapter, refers to two people experiencing grief in different ways. Grief is a universal experience that has no one-size-fits-all solution for partners. Every person has their own way of coping with loss, which can cause tension between partners who approach grief differently. Neither partner's view is wrong; differences in coping styles are simply that, differences, and should be respected and accepted by both parties. That said, it can still be challenging to understand each other's perspective.

Incongruent grieving styles between partners can lead to what experts refer to as a secondary loss—a stressful shift in the previous relationship.

Couples might face difficulties with intimacy, communication, and even day-to-day functioning. Frustration can cause partners to blame each other for the loss, intensifying any existing conflict. On top of that, pre-existing challenges in the relationship can be magnified by the stress of the loss, leading partners to fight about issues that have been bothering them. Even a solid relationship can fracture under the strain of this challenging life event.

> *We had been trying for months to get pregnant. When it ended in a loss, we had a hard time grappling with the emotional fallout, which immensely strained our relationship. Petty arguments and disagreements suddenly seemed to be more frequent and intense than before. We argued about who did what chores around the house or what to watch on TV. Even though these issues were minor, they seemed to carry much more weight in light of our stress.*
>
> *I'm grateful for my wife's willingness to try and mend our relationship during such a difficult period. We decided that if we wanted to make it through this together, we would need to put extra effort into understanding and communicating more lovingly with each other and rebuilding our actual friendship and bond. Together, we have managed to stay strong.*
>
> —Dwayne, 34

Same-sex couples face unique challenges with incongruent grief after a pregnancy loss. One significant issue is the societal perception that the loss primarily impacts the birthing parent. As a result, the non-birthing partner's grief is overlooked. The difference in support from others toward the birthing parent can create tension in the relationship between the partners. When both partners are non-birthing, the lack of physical connection to the pregnancy can lead to varying degrees of emotional attachment and different levels of grief. For example, one partner may have been more emotionally invested in the pregnancy, perhaps due to being a genetic contributor. The loss may have a more profound impact on them compared to their partner. The differences in their grief can lead to feelings of isolation or resentment, which can strain their relationship—ultimately creating a divide when mutual support is most needed.

So, how can partners cope with incongruent grief? The first step is acknowledging and respecting each other's feelings and perspectives. It's okay if you and your partner don't feel the same way; what matters most is that you recognize and validate each other's emotions. One way to do this is by actively listening to one another. We shouldn't interrupt or deny each other's perspective. By paying close attention to what the other person is saying, including their tone of voice and body language, we can gain insight into their feelings and acknowledge that we understand and respect them—even if we have a different view.

Even physical contact, like holding hands or embracing, can be a powerful way to demonstrate support and understanding.

Another helpful strategy is seeking support outside of your relationship. Joining a support group for parents who have experienced a loss can provide a safe space for sharing your feelings and connecting with others who understand what you're going through. Not only can this lend emotional support and guidance, but it may also help you to cultivate genuine relationships where you can mutually hold one another accountable.

An effective exercise for finding common ground can be sitting with your backs together and having an open dialogue. This allows both people to share their feelings without any visual distractions or cues that could be disruptive. Not only does this provide emotional support for each partner, but it also offers a unique opportunity for physical connection.

We've stressed the significance of self-care many times throughout this guidebook, but here's one more reminder: you must prioritize your mental health and practice self-care as you navigate through grief. Regularly take time for yourself, whether it's through exercise, setting boundaries, or simply engaging in enjoyable activities. The benefits are endless.

Lastly, if needed, seek professional help. A therapist or counselor can assist partners in effectively communicating with each other and provide skills to manage challenging emotions such as anger, bitterness, and grief that may arise from loss. They can also help identify triggers for negative feelings and develop strategies to cope with them.

Working through incongruent grief can be a daunting task. Still, it's possible to make significant progress when both partners are committed to understanding and supporting each other. By acknowledging and respecting each other's feelings, seeking support outside the relationship, and practicing self-care, partners can discover new ways of navigating the grieving process and develop an even stronger bond.

Supporting Your Partner

Now equipped with the knowledge of how to care for yourself, a deeper understanding of your emotional support needs, and better preparation for coping with incongruent grief, you're in a better position to support your partner. Here are twelve suggestions for ways to get started:

1. **Encourage Self-Care**. Loss can be an incredibly isolating experience for many people, and it's common to miss out on even the basic needs like eating regularly and getting enough sleep. Encouraging your partner to prioritize self-care by engaging in activities they enjoy (even briefly) or suggesting calming activities like deep breathing exercises or walking outdoors could help ease some of their tension.

2. **Offer Practical Support**. Simple tasks like making meals, running errands, doing laundry, etc., can remove some of their burdens

when they lack the energy or motivation for these tasks themselves. Additionally, consider setting reminders for doctor's appointments or other necessary tasks related to their healing process so they don't have the added stress around forgetting something important.

3. **Put in the effort to understand your partner's preferred emotional support style**. Do they need a cheerleader? A listener? A rock? Learning about their preferences can help you give them the comfort and understanding they require. Be sure to communicate your preferred style so that you can support each other effectively.

4. **Engage in exercises that strengthen the bond between you and your partner**. For instance, try picking a support style for the day and practicing it. If your partner says they need affection, provide them with that support. On the other hand, if they want to vent without feeling judged, listen attentively and offer empathy.

5. **Be aware that certain dates or occasions may bring up difficult emotions related to the loss**. These can include the day your baby was due, the anniversary of the loss, religious holidays like Christmas, or even Mother's Day and Father's Day. Know that on these days, your partner may need additional support.

6. **Don't feel like you have to know the right thing to say**. Even if you don't know what to say or if they don't want to talk, simply sitting together in silence can be comforting. Active listening can significantly affect how your partner copes with their grief.

7. **Create a safe space.** Be present and listen to your partner without judging or interrupting them. This will help them feel safe to express how they feel.

8. **Make it a priority to take some time apart as individuals**. Space can be good for processing and coping with what you are going through.

9. **Take time to come together**. Checking in with each other is an opportunity to vent and open up. Make room for meaningful conversations that will bring you closer as a couple while building a solid connection. You can also add fun activities like watching a favorite TV show together.

10. **Create Rituals and Memorials Together**. Collaborating on rituals or memorials to honor the loss can be a healing experience and provide a shared space for remembrance and reflection.

11. **Practice the Power of Touch**. Providing physical comfort, such as hugs, cuddling, or holding hands, can offer solace and a sense of security.

12. **Adopt a teamwork mentality**. Instead of feeling isolated in your private battle with grief, approach it with your partner as a united front, viewing the journey ahead as a "we" and not solely as an individual experience. This approach will allow you to comfort and be compassionate with each other. It also creates a connection that's otherwise absent when going solo.

Conclusion

Remember that as a partner, you have an equal right to process your pain, receive comfort and understanding from those around you, and grieve—regardless of your gender. Knowing this puts you in an even better position to be support*ed* and be support*ive*.

Rest Stop

1. **Take a moment to reflect**. Write down a lesson from this chapter that will help guide your way, like understanding and communicating your preferred style of emotional support.

2. **Take the *Crawl. Walk. Run. Soar.* self-assessment:**

   How are you feeling today? (circle one)

   Crawling – Making small but determined actions on your path to healing.

   Walking – Building momentum and making steady, consistent progress.

   Running – Taking rapid strides despite challenges.

   Soaring – Reaching new heights as you move forward toward an optimistic future.

   Remember: One day, you may soar, and the next, you may crawl. And that's okay. Healing isn't a linear journey with a set destination. It is continual progress toward feeling better.

3. **Take a break**. Give your mind a well-deserved break, then come back fresh and ready to dive into the next chapter tomorrow.

Notes

Chapter 7
Sharing the News with Others

Many cultures around the world have distinct views on when to announce a pregnancy. In some cultures, it should be announced as soon as possible to receive blessings from the community. In other regions, like the United States, society traditionally dictates that parents wait until after the first trimester before sharing the news. It can be a difficult wait, filled with anxiety and uncertainty, but one that many view as necessary to spare parents from publicly mourning a loss. This waiting period is primarily for the protection of parents-to-be since the risk of loss is highest during early pregnancy.

Although this approach may have its advantages, ultimately, it comes at a cost. By not openly sharing their loss stories, those who have been through it, often feel isolated in their grief. Since their typical support systems are unaware of the situation, they aren't able to provide the deserved support. Oftentimes, it's not until after sharing our own loss experience that we realize how many people in our lives have had a similar experience. When we don't share our losses, we miss the opportunity for this shared connection and the therapeutic benefits of verbally processing the physical and emotional pain involved.

At the same time, we must acknowledge the importance of creating an environment where everyone feels safe to share their experience without fear of judgment or criticism. Open conversations can reduce the stigma surrounding it and provide comfort for those going through similar struggles in silence. And if nothing else, by speaking out, we can remind ourselves just how resilient and capable each of us is.

On the other hand, many people prefer to keep their story of loss private for various valid reasons. Some people delay sharing their experience until they're ready to discuss it openly. Sharing such news can evoke strong emotions; understandably, some prefer to process them away from public scrutiny. Similarly, those who choose to grieve privately may feel anxious about how others might perceive the news. It can be especially upsetting if the loss isn't fully understood or viewed the same way. While the decision to keep the loss private may seem unorthodox or secretive, it should never be considered wrong or selfish; instead, it's just one of the many healing paths a person may take.

No matter your chosen path, you must know there is no one-size-fits-all approach. The decision of whether or not to share your story is yours and should be based on what feels suitable to you.

In this chapter, we'll dig into the different factors you should consider before making your decision and how to prepare for delivering the news. We'll also share practical guidance on what to say and how to communicate the news effectively to adults and children. Additionally, we'll delve into the reactions that might follow and give you tips on how to manage them. So, if you're struggling with whether or not to share your pregnancy loss with your loved ones or wondering how to approach the conversation, this chapter has you covered.

Is sharing the news right for you?

Here are some things you can consider to help you arrive at your decision of whether or not to share:

Sharing the news isn't mandatory

If someone were already aware of your pregnancy, you would likely want to update them on how it ended. However, if someone wasn't privy to the pregnancy, you shouldn't feel obligated to share the news with them. Consider that sharing big news all at once—announcing both the pregnancy and loss—could be overwhelming for some people who weren't previously aware of your situation. Even under those circumstances, close relationships would likely still want to know.

Ultimately, arriving at your decision to share could be a matter of updating those who already knew about the pregnancy on its progress and not sharing the information with those who didn't know about it. Remember, this is a personal decision, and there is no right or wrong way to handle it.

Why do you want to share?

Understanding your reasons for sharing the news of your loss can help you arrive at your decision. Is it because you feel obligated to share? Are you sharing to seek empathy or to connect with those closest to you? Maybe you want to seek guidance on the path ahead. Or it could be that you just need someone to listen. Whatever your "why" may be, taking the time to understand it and its benefits will help you decide whether you want to share this part of your story.

Consider whom you will share the news with

Notify your doctor immediately to schedule a check-up and any necessary testing. After that, depending on your relationship, family is often the first call when you want to share life updates. Friends are the next logical choice as they can provide empathy and help with practical tasks like taking care of household chores or errands you may not feel up to doing yourself.

Some people find it helpful to share their experiences in private groups on social media platforms because it's an outlet for sharing in a place where people understand it. Some parents share the news with their co-workers since they may have a close group they feel comfortable with at work. Others share the news with those who can offer spiritual or religious guidance or support. When sharing the news of your loss, consider who will provide support and understanding. Ultimately, they should be your first consideration.

Are you prepared to address the loss with a child?

When expecting a new sibling, children often become invested in the preparations and anticipation of their arrival. Consider whether you want to involve your child in the conversation. Even if they were unaware of the pregnancy, your child may have recognized something is wrong. By addressing the loss in an age-appropriate way, you can give them insight and understanding into what's happened. This approach can also help lessen any concerns and be a good opportunity to teach them healthy coping strategies.

Are you prepared to deal with people's reactions?

Before sharing your loss, consider whether you feel prepared to deal with people's reactions. Think about the individual(s) you plan to share the news with and whether they will likely offer support or say something insensitive due to ignorance or differing views. Also, consider whether they have a history of receiving difficult news well or if their response may emotionally overwhelm you. Considering these factors can help you determine if and when to share the news with them.

You don't have to share your news right away

Take some time. Then you may feel more prepared to have a conversation and manage any reactions. Right now, you are the priority.

What if you and your partner disagree on which approach to take?

It had been two weeks since our miscarriage, and the pain still ran deep. I wanted nothing more than to share about the pregnancy, the loss, and the subsequent pain I was going through with our closest friends and family. I needed to find solace in the love of those who surrounded me. But whenever I brought it up, James disagreed.

He had always been one to deal with problems in private to shield himself from prying eyes and unwanted attention. He argued that we didn't have to share everything with our loved ones. He felt it was better to deal with it in the intimacy of our home, just between us.

I know that everyone handles grief differently and that he deserves to have the space he needs to cope. But I still felt how I felt. As our conversations went in circles, we grew frustrated with each other. Our points of view were valid, but we just couldn't find common ground.

Then one day, over a bowl of chips and salsa on our patio, I proposed something to James. I suggested I would tell only my mom and sisters and no one else. To my surprise, James was open to the idea. But he felt it still wouldn't work. My mom can't keep a secret to save her life—her knowing about it was the equivalent of blasting it on the national news.

Eventually, we came up with a compromise: I would share the news with my mom and sisters and send an email updating our families on what happened. Sharing the news this way meant we wouldn't have to talk about it in person, which is what James had most wanted to avoid in the first place. Thankfully, this option worked well. In the email, I set boundaries and stated our need for space to grieve and heal. James was relieved that at family events, he wasn't barraged by people asking how he was doing or giving him hugs that would stir up emotions he didn't want to deal with in public.

In finding our own happy medium, we were able to respect each other's grieving processes and get the support and space we needed.

—Michelle, 33

If you and your partner can't agree on whether to share your news, consult a neutral third party such as a religious leader, relationship counselor, qualified mediator, or couples support group. They can help you find a happy medium.

Additional Considerations

Parents who experience a loss of a desired pregnancy due to termination for maternal health or fetal anomaly may be more likely to keep their loss a secret for fear of judgment or criticism of such a highly debated issue. While they unquestionably have the right to make this choice, they should do so knowing that concealing such a significant life event may inadvertently create tension in family interactions, as the strain of maintaining secrecy can lead to feelings of disconnect or isolation. These parents should consider seeking outside support from an objective party, such as a therapist or counselor, to help cope with the emotional impact.

In cases of infant loss, it's usually not a question of whether to share the news, as most people would have known about the pregnancy or even met the baby. Instead, these parents' focus would be on how to deliver the news sensitively and appropriately. We will cover this in detail in the next section.

Preparing to Deliver the News

If you choose to be open about your experience with loss, you should prepare before having the conversation. Being proactive can help create an emotionally secure space for everyone involved.

Think about your preferred method of communication. For some, having a conversation in person or over the phone is the most comfortable option. In contrast, others may opt for sending a text message as it can be easier to express difficult information this way. Alternatively, sharing your story on social media can be an easy way to update a larger circle of people in one go; however, this impersonal approach may cause some hurt feelings and offense. Consider all aspects before making a decision that works best for you.

Once you've decided how to deliver the message, reflect on what you want to say and how you feel about it. Writing down your thoughts can help organize them and ensure that you express yourself clearly during the conversation.

Consider how much detail you feel comfortable sharing about your experience and establish any necessary boundaries, such as whether the person should keep the news private. Setting boundaries will help you clarify what you feel comfortable discussing and what's off-limits. You can decide whether to give a full account of your story or simply inform the person of your loss without continuing the discussion. Being aware of your preference ahead of time can help you guide the conversation.

If you're uncomfortable communicating the message, consider relying on a trusted family member or close friend to relay it for you. A helper can ease some of the emotional burden and allow you to focus on taking care of yourself. Having someone else deliver the news can also be a good way to establish boundaries and let others know if you need some space.

What to Say and How to Say It—to Adults

Now that you have a plan, it's time to deliver the news. We have created the following five-step process to help make it a little easier:

1. Be gentle and honest when delivering the news of your loss. Use language that conveys your feelings and the fact of the matter. A good way to start could be, "I have some difficult news to share with you. We recently lost our baby due to [the reason], and we are heartbroken." Use words that accurately explain what happened, like miscarriage or stillbirth, instead of euphemisms like "went away" or "passed on." If you'd rather not be so specific, a simple explanation such as, "We ran into some complications, and I lost the baby," is sufficient.

2. The other person will likely need to process the news. Allow them space and time to take it in, and don't feel pressured to fill any awkward silence with words.

3. You can then share as much or as little as you're comfortable with regarding the circumstances of your loss and answer questions you're okay answering. Let the other person know if you've reached your limit. You could say, "I'd rather not get into any further specifics because everything is so raw, but I wanted to let you know what happened." Communicating your boundaries allows you to move on to whatever you prefer to talk about next.

4. This is a good time to let them know how much their support would mean to you in the coming days. Directly express the type of support you need. Whether it's them being your cheerleader or helping hand around the house, let them know what specific actions they can take that would be most impactful for you. Check out Chapter 8 to learn more about the different types of support and ways your supporters can demonstrate them.

5. Lastly, you can share the coping strategies you're relying on to get through this. After all, when a child is lost, it isn't just the parents who are impacted; friends and family members are also likely to be emotionally affected. Talking about your coping strategies may help them too. Coping together can be a good way to get through this period of grief as a group, not just individually.

When it's time to deliver your news, remember: be gentle and honest; allow the other person to process the news; share additional details you want to share; let them know ways to support you; and share coping strategies that have helped you and may help them.

There are additional considerations for sharing your news in the workplace.

Communicating the News:
Decide how you want to communicate the news to your colleagues or superiors, such as through an email to your boss, a private meeting with your team, or a phone conversation with human resources. Remember, it's up to you how much detail you want to share.

Interacting with Colleagues:
Colleagues may not always know how to respond appropriately to your loss. It might be helpful to let them know what kind of support you need. For example, you might say, "I appreciate your condolences. Right now, I find comfort in focusing on work. Thanks for understanding." Or, "It's okay if you'd like to ask me about my experience. I'd appreciate a listening ear."

Requesting Time Off:
Taking time off work can be instrumental in your healing process. Many companies offer bereavement leave. Unfortunately, this leave does not always cover pregnancy loss. According to the U.S. Department of Labor, *The Family and Medical Leave Act* (*FMLA*) provides certain employees with up to twelve

weeks of unpaid, job-protected leave per year. However, time off with no pay may not be financially possible for many employees. You might consider using sick leave or vacation days if available. To request time off, you could say, "Due to a personal loss, I will need some time off to grieve and recover." Be aware that for certain companies, time-off requests may need to be accompanied by a doctor's note or specific documents.

Managing People's Reactions

We wanted to title this section *Stupid People: Navigating a World Where People Say Stupid Things and Don't Understand Your Grief*. But we have more tact than that.

Unfortunately, people don't always react to the news of our loss in the way that we hoped they would. Some common reactions include trying to comfort you by saying things like, "You can just have another baby," or offering advice to "move on with your life." Others may refuse to talk about death or provide any support. Some people will compare their experiences to yours or give their opinion on what you should do next.

People's reactions to loss vary depending on their background, culture, religious beliefs, and life experiences. By understanding how these factors play into people's responses, we can better come to terms with some of the less-than-desirable reactions.

Try to remember that your family and friends may not know what to say or do when you tell them about your loss; they could just be trying to help in the best way they know how. That doesn't mean that their reactions are ones that you feel comfortable with. If they don't respond in a supportive way, give them pointers on what would be more helpful.

For example, you might say, "I disagree with your comment that 'God causes things to happen for a reason.' I find it hurtful that you would imply God took my baby from me. I know you're only trying to help, and I appreciate your support. Rather than platitudes, I need a listening ear right now."

Being clear on where you stand will help them avoid making insensitive comments and direct their support toward more meaningful actions.

When it comes to unsolicited advice, if you're not open to receiving it, you can acknowledge what's been said but then take back control of the conversation. Doing this will give you a sense of authority and help to prevent feeling overwhelmed by other people's opinions. You could say, "I'm not really looking for advice right now, but I'll let you know if that changes, and I would welcome any suggestions."

Some people respond to loss by relating it to an experience they've been through. While their intention may be to connect with you, it can come across as overshadowing your story with their own. If someone continues to talk about their own story of loss when you're trying to share yours, it's okay and appropriate to direct the conversation back to yourself. For example, you could say, "It sounds like you've gone through something similar, and I'm sorry that happened to you. Can we get back to my story for now?"

Just because one person feels comfortable talking about their loss doesn't mean everyone does. If someone constantly brings up a conversation that is too painful for you, let them know that you need some time away from talking about it and that when you're ready, you will discuss it with them. You could say, "I appreciate you giving me space to talk about this, but I'm just not up for it. I'll know exactly who I can go to when and if I ever am."

If someone's emotional reaction is too overwhelming for you, kindly tell them to take some space to manage their feelings and that you need to do the same. You can say, "I know how tough this is for you, and I'm feeling overwhelmed too. Let's both take a break before we talk further about this." You can revisit the conversation when both of you feel more emotionally stable.

Respect the capability of your family and friends regarding how much or how little support they are willing to offer. Even if you long for their help in particular ways, you must recognize that they will only do what their capacity allows. Don't consider their limitations to be a reflection of your relationship with them; instead, it's simply a personal ability or boundary. Accept what they can do and get support from other sources in areas they aren't able or willing to.

Everybody reacts differently when receiving the news of a pregnancy or infant loss. What's most important is that you feel confident in your capacity to cope well regardless of what reactions are expressed by those around you.

What to Say and How to Say It—to Children

Children understand death and grief in different ways based on their age. When talking about loss, we should be honest with them and explain it in a way they can understand. This will help create a safe environment to talk about how they feel.

Here are some examples of what to say and how to say it, depending on a child's age.

Zero to two years (infants and toddlers)

When a family member dies, babies can sense the emotions of the people around them, even if they don't have the words to express their feelings. Conversation might not be the best approach to helping them understand what's happened. Instead, try things like memory-making activities and include them in your healthy coping habits, like going for a walk. Simply cuddling for physical comfort and reassurance can make a difference too.

Three to five years (pre-schoolers)

Explaining death to a young child can be easier if you use books with pictures. After reading, explain that their sibling is "dead" or has "died," meaning they won't see them again. The child might think death isn't permanent, so you may need to explain it more than once. They might also think it's because of something bad they did. Give them lots of love and reassurance that they're not to blame.

Using direct words like dead and died instead of phrases like "passed away" and "in a better place" will cut down on confusion and help avoid uncomfortable follow-up questions like "Why was here not a good enough place for them?" You might lead the conversation by saying, "I want to talk to you about something important that has happened in our family. You know how Mommy was carrying your little brother or sister in her belly, and we were all waiting to meet them? Well, they won't be coming to join our family like we thought. They didn't grow enough, which means they died and won't be able to join our family."

When they ask why this happened, a further explanation could be, "Sometimes babies don't grow the way they're supposed to. You didn't do anything wrong to make this happen; no one did. It's okay to feel sad about this; Mommy and Daddy do too. They may not be here with us, but we can still remember them and keep their memory in our hearts."

They may ask questions like, "Did the baby go to heaven?" It's best to respond thoughtfully. You could say, "I believe they are somewhere where it's beautiful, and they aren't in any pain—and they know how much you, Mommy, and Daddy love them." Sharing your optimistic beliefs will help to shape their impressionable views. This age group may be more likely to ask a rapid-fire series of questions. It's impossible to predict what their little minds will come up with. Try to answer as thoughtfully as possible and remember that "I don't know" can be an honest and accurate response. While you may not know the answer to a specific question, what you do know is that you love them and will be there for them through any challenges they face. Offer this reassurance to them.

Ways to support them:

- If they cry, let them know that crying is okay. Be there to comfort them.

- Plant an indoor flower in honor of their sibling and teach them how to take care of it.

- Have them draw a pretty picture for their sibling.

- Continue to read books on loss.

- Keep their routine the same; consistency will help create a sense of stability.

- Consult a pediatrician or other healthcare professional if you feel they are not coping well. Telltale signs are behaviors like acting out, bedwetting, or withdrawing from activities they enjoy.

Six to eight years (middle childhood)

Guiding young hearts through the topic of death can be delicate, but with tender care, we can help middle-aged children grasp its meaning. First, use concrete language to describe the loss. You might say, "I want to talk with you about something important that happened. I was pregnant, which meant I had a baby growing inside my belly. But I had a miscarriage. This means that the baby we were expecting isn't going to be part of our family anymore because it died. Sometimes, we don't know exactly why a miscarriage happens, but it's important to remember that it's no one's fault. It's just a part of the natural process that sometimes happens. You and I, and everyone in our family, can still love and cherish the memory of the baby we lost, and we can talk about our feelings together."

It's okay to ask them if they understand. Follow their lead and gently correct any misinformation. Also, leave room for them to engage in play and creativity, as these could be ways they express what they can't put into words.

Ways to support them:

- Let them engage in physical activities like going to the playground or tossing a ball around.

- Incorporate age-appropriate books about grief or death into reading time.
- Be open to having conversations if they show curiosity.
- Consult a pediatrician or other healthcare professional if you feel they are not coping well. Telltale signs include acting out, bedwetting, or withdrawing from activities they enjoy.

Nine to twelve years (preteen)

Preteens may grapple with how it will impact their lives after a sibling's death. Reassure them by maintaining their familiar routines and be an example for them of coping with grief in a healthy way. Share your emotions and strategies for healing, but steer clear of imposing your feelings onto them—they may not view the loss the same way as you. Respect their boundaries when discussing the loss, but keep communication open when they're ready to share.

The conversation might look something like, "I want to talk with you about something sad that happened recently to our family. You know that your baby sister was due to be born soon. I went to the doctor to check on the baby, and tests showed that her heart stopped beating. This is called a stillbirth, which means that the baby died before being born. Sometimes, even doctors don't have all the answers for why things like this happen.

"In the upcoming days and weeks, you might see me or your dad feeling sad or even crying, and it's because we are grieving the death of your baby sister. But we'll make sure to be there for you too. We will continue our everyday routines, like going to school and spending time together as a family. We can talk about it if you want, but if you don't feel like it right now, that's okay too. I will be here if and when you do."

Ways to support them:

- Stick to routines.
- Encourage physical activity and exercise.

- Create a playlist of music they enjoy.
- Let them help you with memorial activities, like creating a memory box or memory bracelet or releasing lanterns in honor of their sibling.
- Give them a journal and let them do a brain dump about their feelings.
- Read age-appropriate books on death and grief.
- Consult a pediatrician or other healthcare professional if you feel they are not coping well. Telltale signs are behaviors like hostility, defiance, or out-of-character meltdowns.

Thirteen to eighteen years (teens and young adults)

As you share the news of your loss with your teen or young adult child, be ready to navigate deep and thought-provoking questions about life, spirituality, or how to make sense of tragedy. While you may not have all the answers to their questions, your willingness to explore them together—with empathy and honesty—is enough. However, don't be offended if they open up to their friends or another family member instead of you. What matters is that they have the supportive ear they need.

You might start the conversation by saying, "There's something I need to tell you that is really hard for me to say. [Baby's name] died last night in his sleep. The doctors said it was sudden infant death syndrome. There's not really a known cause, and there was nothing anyone could have done. I know how much you loved your baby brother and how excited you were to watch him grow up. This is an unimaginable loss for our family. But we will get through this together, even though it may not seem that way right now. I'm here for you if you want to talk about how you're feeling."

Ways to support them:

- Stick to routines but be ready to pivot if they need space and time to grieve.

- Allow them to have social time with friends and do activities they enjoy.
- Give them a journal and let them do a brain dump about their feelings.
- Read age-appropriate books on death and grief.
- Connect them with support groups online or in person if needed.
- Consult a pediatrician or other healthcare professional if you feel they are not coping well. Telltale signs include poor school performance, social withdrawal, or lack of enthusiasm or motivation.

Conclusion

The decision to share the news of a pregnancy or infant loss ultimately lies in our hands. If we choose to share this news, we should do it in a considerate and empathetic way. Preparing for the conversation and managing people's reactions can help make the conversation go well for you and them.

Rest Stop

1. **Take a moment to reflect**. Write down a lesson from this chapter that will help guide your way, like how you can prepare to discuss your loss.

2. **Take the *Crawl. Walk. Run. Soar.* self-assessment:**

    How are you feeling today? (circle one)

    Crawling – Making small but determined actions on your path to healing.

Walking – Building momentum and making steady, consistent progress.

Running – Taking rapid strides despite challenges.

Soaring – Reaching new heights as you move forward toward an optimistic future.

Remember: One day, you may soar, and the next, you may crawl. And that's okay. Healing isn't a linear journey with a set destination. It is continual progress toward feeling better.

3. **Take a break**. Give your mind a well-deserved break, then come back fresh and ready to dive into the next chapter tomorrow.

Notes

Part Three

Learning to Live without Them: Navigating Life while Coping

Chapter 8
Accepting ~~Help~~ Support

When my hair started falling out from stress, I realized I couldn't continue coping with my baby's loss alone. I had to learn how to accept support from the people around me, and it was an incredibly humbling experience. I had been shutting everyone out, but now it was clear I needed them. When I opened up about what I had been going through, my friends and family immediately took action. They helped get my other kids to and from school, cooked large batches of food, and listened when I needed to vent; my colleagues even took work tasks off my to-do list. Their support enabled me to carry on and take better care of myself. I truly appreciated the power of their collective support and have learned (the hard way) just how important it is to lean on the people around me.

—Asha, 38

This chapter was originally titled "Accepting *Help*." But we changed the verbiage due to the negative connotations associated with the word "help." Even the seemingly harmless phrase "you need help" is often weaponized and used to undercut others. Being in a position where you need help can often be viewed as a sign of instability or weakness and is usually seen as something to be avoided or hidden. In today's society, there is an idealization of being independent and strong enough to not need any aid from anyone else. This way of thinking leaves many feeling ashamed and embarrassed when they need outside assistance, making the concept of "asking for help" one that can spark anxiety and apprehension.

So, we made the change to the word "support." Support is an essential element of relationships, defined as the act of providing assistance and encouragement. It involves being there for someone, listening to their concerns, and helping them work through difficult situations. Support can come in many forms, such as emotional, informational, financial, and practical, which we will explore more in the upcoming section. By accepting support from others, we are courageously embracing a valuable resource that empowers us to cope well.

In this chapter, we'll define your circle of support and explore how they can best support you. Then we'll provide suggestions for how to get what you need if you don't have a built-in support network. Lastly, we'll discuss the benefits of seeking professional support and provide tips for finding a good-fit relationship with a therapist or counselor.

Defining Your Circle and Ways They Can Support You

Studies have found that those who don't have access to emotional support are more likely to suffer from depression and anxiety than those who do. In addition, having a network of people to talk to and lean on reduces feelings of isolation. It helps us effectively manage our emotions. Access to a compassionate community can also help decrease overall stress levels, which is also beneficial for physical health. It's clear that surrounding ourselves with people who intentionally offer their support is necessary.

In Chapter 6, we talked about distinctive support styles in which those around us are likely to demonstrate their support: the comforter, the problem-solver, the cheerleader, the listener, and the rock. These are the people you feel comfortable talking to and who will be there for you when you need them.

Take a moment to write a list of these people in your life. Your circle of support can include your partner, family members, friends, co-workers, or anyone you feel close to and know you can count on.

Once you've identified your support network, figure out how they can assist you. Asking for support is usually difficult for many of us—we don't want to appear needy or burden those around us. So we choose to suffer in silence instead. But the people who love you don't want that; they want to make a difference.

Here are four types of support and ways the folks in your circle can demonstrate them:

Practical Support:

Even the most mundane tasks can feel like overwhelming obstacles when navigating our grief after a pregnancy loss. During these moments, practical support from family and friends can make a difference. Things like looking after other children, preparing meals/ordering takeout, or running our errands, allow us to prioritize our well-being and focus more on our healing.

Emotional Support:

There are a myriad of ways your supporters can show emotional support:

By acknowledging your loss

They can acknowledge your loss by validating your feelings about it. They should avoid making comments that downplay the significance of your experience or minimize your grief, such as, "Well, you can always adopt another baby," or "At least you have other children."

By being a judgment-free zone

When your supporters are willing to listen with understanding and an open mind, it provides a safe, non-judgmental space for you to express your thoughts and feelings about your loss.

By educating themselves on your type of loss

They may benefit from learning more about the loss you experienced. Resources such as books, blogs, and articles can give them a better understanding of what you are going through so they can support you more effectively during your conversations.

By respecting your privacy

They should respect your privacy after a loss. If you don't want to talk about it, they should respect your wishes and not press you for details.

By being patient

Everyone deals with grief in their own way. Your supporters can demonstrate patience by honoring the best pace and approach for you.

By being there for the long haul

They should not only be there for you immediately after your loss but throughout the hard road that follows. Having supportive friends who will stick by you for all the milestones, anniversaries, and triggering moments ahead can make a difference when you need it most.

Informational Support:

Let your supporters know if you are open to receiving helpful informational resources like books, online forums, support groups, and websites. Sharing these resources can be an excellent way for them to show their support and can reduce the amount of work it takes for you to find this information on your own.

Financial Support:

After a loss, there may be financial burdens to consider, such as funeral or other expenses. Some people might be unable to support you in other ways, but they would still be happy to provide financial assistance. Let them help if they can.

Earlier, you compiled a list of your support network. Now, you don't have to wrack your brain when they say, "Let me know what I can do to help." Instead, you have permission to accept their support and confidently refer to the list above for tangible ways they can show it.

Here is some verbiage you can use as a starting point:

Practical Support: *I've been really low on energy lately, so if you want to drop off a meal or order delivery, that would really be helpful.*

Emotional Support: *Right now, I just need some time to process everything. When I'm ready to talk, having you by my side would be great. In the meantime, if you want to send some funny memes, it would make me smile.*

Informational Support: *I'm looking to connect with other parents who have gone through similar experiences, but I don't know where to start. It would be helpful if you could look into some options for me. I'm open to connecting either in person or online.*

Financial Support: *This loss completely took us aback, and we are trying to raise funds to cover the burial and a memorial service. If you'd like to contribute toward this, we would greatly appreciate it.*

Getting Support When You Don't Have a Support Network

Following a loss, some of us realize we don't have the support network we thought we would have. We often expect family and friends to be the most supportive, but unfortunately, this isn't always the case. Loved ones sometimes fail to understand or sympathize with our pain, and even those who want to provide support may not have the emotional capacity for it. This lack of support can leave us feeling lonely, confused, betrayed, and desperate for comfort.

> *My early miscarriage was awful, but what made it worse was that none of my family or friends understood how hard it was on me—not even my partner. No one got why I was so upset because it hadn't been real to them yet; they hadn't heard the baby's heartbeat or felt the reminders of its presence from swollen breasts and morning sickness like I had. The loss wasn't as big a deal to them, but it was a really big emotional blow for me.*
>
> *It took a lot of effort for me not to become bitter. I'm proud that I managed to find the courage to seek outside support to cope with my loss despite the lack of understanding from the people around me.*
>
> —Shauna, 34

Even though you may not find support from the people you're expecting it from, other options are still available.

Practical Support:

One way to get practical support when you don't have a support network is to seek local non-profit organizations that provide food assistance, legal aid, and financial counseling. Additionally, there may be government programs available to assist you. An Internet search for the area of practical support you're looking for can help you locate organizations in your area.

Emotional Support:

It can be difficult not having a friend or family member to turn to for emotional support when it's needed most. Many find comfort in joining online communities with people who are going through the same experiences. These groups offer a safe space to express ourselves without judgment or fear of being misunderstood. Online forums are also great for finding resources such as counseling services, in-person support groups, and other forms of assistance.

Informational Support:

Libraries are a great resource for informational support since they typically offer free access to books, magazines, newspapers, and other media-related materials that can help expand knowledge on pregnancy and infant loss. Public libraries may also provide computer stations where you can access the Internet to do research.

Financial Support:

Having limited financial resources doesn't mean help is out of reach. There are options available to assist with final arrangements, such as The TEARS Foundation, state departments that offer public assistance, and local funeral homes. You can do an online search to find additional local or national options.

Accepting Support from a Professional

While relying on friends and self-help resources can be beneficial, it may not always be enough. When things get overwhelming, seeking the guidance of a professional can make an incredible difference.

With personalized attention and a customized treatment plan specific to your unique needs, a counselor or therapist can help you explore your emotions, gain valuable insights, and develop healthy coping strategies you may not have considered. Needing additional support is not a sign of weakness. Sometimes, seeking support is the bravest thing you can do for yourself.

> *I never could have imagined going through the grief I did when my baby died. Nothing prepared me for it, not even all of the motivational and inspirational books lining my shelves or all the support and love from my friends and family. I was in a deep, dark place that I just couldn't seem to get out of.*
>
> *One day, out of sheer desperation, I contacted a professional therapist. As a Black woman in my community, this was terribly taboo and frowned upon. "You're a strong Black woman; you can handle this," people said to me over and over. But I knew that if I didn't do more than just hope and pray the pain away, I would continue to spiral mentally and eventually break.*
>
> *At first, talking with someone who wasn't part of my inner circle about such a personal experience felt strange. I wasn't used to doing that with strangers. But as time went by, with each session, I noticed the pain I'd been carrying seemed less intense until it eventually felt like the clouds were parting and life was returning to me.*
>
> *My therapist became an invaluable confidant throughout this journey. She gave me insight and tools for navigating my turbulent emotions, which helped me confront them head-on instead of running away from them like I always had in the past. She also gave me unconditional support and understanding in ways nobody else could.*

I'm glad I chose to take the leap and reach out for professional assistance. Now I really am a strong Black woman—one with a strong, supportive therapist in my corner.

—Nicole, 33

Here is some guidance on finding and building a good-fit relationship with a professional counselor or therapist:

You should first understand the difference between a counselor and a therapist to know which option may be better for you. Counselors focus more on helping clients build coping skills to manage specific present-day issues like anxiety or depression. On the other hand, therapists take a more comprehensive approach that focuses on examining the client's history, past experiences, and thought patterns to uncover any underlying causes that may be contributing to a current emotional crisis. Both can be effective in grief counseling. It's just a matter of which approach you prefer.

Begin your search by reaching out to your primary care physician, who may be able to provide a referral to a qualified grief specialist in your area. You can also search online directories such as Psychology Today or GoodTherapy.org, which allow you to search based on location and specialty. Additionally, many hospitals offer bereavement services, including counselors and therapists experienced in grief counseling. Finally, consider contacting non-profit organizations like The Women's Center of Southeast Michigan that provide therapy and other individualized support services regardless of the ability to pay.

Take your time researching potential providers. Read up on their professional background, credentials, and areas of specialization.

Consider the logistics—how far away they are, what times they offer sessions, what payment methods they accept, etc., and if it works for you.

Do they have a diversity, equity, and inclusion statement? Statements like these can give you insight into how they operate and value their clients.

Ask questions during the initial consultation to get a better sense if the fit is right. Do they have experience with your type of grief? Are they using evidence-based therapy techniques?

When finding a good fit in a provider, approach it like any other relationship. You are seeking someone you can trust, who understands your unique needs, and who can provide support and solid guidance. It may take some time, but don't be afraid to make a change if the relationship doesn't feel right. It's reasonable to explore different options until you find and connect with the right person. If they aren't meeting your specific needs, keep looking and don't settle.

Once you find the right fit and begin your appointments, feeling apprehensive or vulnerable is normal. But, in reality, your provider is just another human being there to support and guide you. So, don't worry about putting up any sort of front or trying to be anything other than yourself. Your provider is there to listen and help you work through your emotions, whatever they may be. It's okay if you don't have everything together or feel like you're struggling more than others might. Your provider isn't there to judge you. So, take a deep breath, relax, and know you're in good hands with someone you have personally vetted.

Conclusion

Having the right support network and relationships can make your experience easier to bear. From establishing a circle of support to reaching out and finding a professional to build a good-fit relationship with, each step can give you the assistance you need—and deserve.

Rest Stop

1. **Take a moment to reflect.** Write down a lesson from this chapter that will help guide your way, like ways you can get support if you don't have a support network.

2. **Take the *Crawl. Walk. Run. Soar.* self-assessment:**

   How are you feeling today? (circle one)

   Crawling – Making small but determined actions on your path to healing.

   Walking – Building momentum and making steady, consistent progress.

   Running – Taking rapid strides despite challenges.

   Soaring – Reaching new heights as you move forward toward an optimistic future.

   Remember: One day, you may soar, and the next, you may crawl. And that's okay. Healing isn't a linear journey with a set destination. It is continual progress toward feeling better.

3. **Take a Break.** Give your mind a well-deserved break, then come back fresh and ready to dive into the next chapter tomorrow.

Notes

Chapter 9
Grief Triggers

After my loss, I desperately wanted all the signs and symptoms of my pregnancy to be gone. But the body doesn't work that way. It has to catch up and realize it's no longer pregnant. Every throbbing ache in my breasts or wave of nausea from my resetting hormones was distressing. Just when I thought I was out of the woods, my period showed up—a cruel reminder that my womb was empty. Month after month, each time I went to the bathroom and saw blood, it sent me into an emotional tailspin and made me feel like I was losing my baby all over again. It was a trigger.

It took me all the days between periods to come to terms with everything happening emotionally. As soon as I'd made progress, it would be time for my period again, sending me right back where I started. I needed to take back my power. I had been through a lot in life, and there was no way I would let my menstrual cycle be the thing that did me in.

So, what did I do? I named my period Angry Bertha. It might sound crazy, but yes, I named it. Then I envisioned what she looked like; a haggard, mean old woman with hormone pimples and painful, swollen breasts. I actually sat down and created a sketch of her. I gave her a messy bun and wilted flowers on her dress. Her fists were balled because she was always grumpy. And she had luggage because she planned to stay at least five days—sometimes six.

After a while, when my period showed up, I would say, "Welcome back, Bertha . . . you old hag!" If I had a bad attitude about something or wanted to binge on sweets, I would tell my husband, "Don't blame me; blame Bertha." It became a running joke that still goes on to this day. Where there were once tears, now there is laughter. I took something that started as a tormenter every month and turned it into something that brought me peace. I reclaimed my power over the trigger.

—Monica, 41

This chapter will outline five types of triggers that can cause grief reactions after a pregnancy or infant loss. While these triggers can be challenging, there are healthy ways to manage them. By the end of this chapter, you will gain insight into how to navigate grief triggers in a way that promotes healing and peace of mind.

Five Types of Grief Triggers

In Chapter 5, we covered four main grief reactions:

- Emotional (sadness, loneliness, mood swings)
- Physical (headaches, high blood pressure, lack of energy)
- Cognitive (difficulty concentrating, bad dreams, excessive thoughts)
- Behavioral (eating too much or too little, ignoring personal hygiene, lack of interest in activities)

A grief trigger causes a person to have a grief reaction. It can be sparked by almost anything: a smell, a feeling, or even certain places. Grief triggers can sneak up on you at any moment, like little time machines that transport you back to an experience. They can happen immediately after a loss or even years later.

For example, you could be managing your day without any major emotional hiccups when suddenly a reminder card arrives in the mail for your baby's upcoming ultrasound—an appointment that would have been scheduled had everything gone according to plan. That reminder sets off an avalanche of feelings, turning what started as a normal day into one filled with emotional unrest.

There are five kinds of grief triggers to be aware of that may trigger a grief reaction.

Sentimental Triggers:

A sentimental trigger is often an object, place, event, or even a date that holds significant emotional value and is closely associated with a person's loss.

I'd been coping pretty well after the loss of our daughter. My goal was to get my wife through it since she was taking it hard. Then one day, I was sitting in my car, stopped at a red light, when my radio began to play "Dance With My Father" by Luther Vandross. Tears started streaming down my face. The lyrics reminded me of what I would now never have: my daughter to dance with at her sweet-sixteen party or on her wedding day. All the feelings I had been shoving aside suddenly came to me all at once, and I grieved the loss of my daughter and all the moments we wouldn't get to share.

—Corey, 40

<u>Physical Triggers</u>:

These can be as simple as breast engorgement or as complex as feeling phantom kicks.

Not only was I mourning the loss of my child, but my body was still recovering from the trauma of childbirth. My doctors prescribed me medicine to help shrink my womb back down, and the sensation of it shrinking felt similar to labor contractions. As each ache overtook my body, I felt like I was reliving the difficult labor all over again. I found myself trembling and crying each time a wave of pain hit. It took some time for me to process that what was happening to my body was part of the healing process and not a continuation of the trauma I'd gone through.

—Jennifer, 26

<u>Environmental Triggers</u>:

Things in your immediate surroundings, such as your baby's room, items they played with, or even the faintest whiff of baby powder, can be enough to trigger a grief reaction.

At six months pregnant, I was standing in my kitchen making smoothies when I started bleeding suddenly and aggressively. My best friend rushed me to the car, and they confirmed at the hospital what I already knew in my heart; I had lost my baby.

When I returned home, the anxiety hit me the second I stepped into the apartment. There was a direct line of sight from the front door to the kitchen where it had all happened, and just looking at that area brought back all of the emotions and fear I felt that day. I stayed at my best friend's place for a few nights because I couldn't stand being in my apartment. Once I finally went back home, it took a couple of weeks before I could go into the kitchen without breaking down in tears or feeling tightness in my chest.

—Shelly, 28

Social Triggers:

Group outings or getting an invite to a baby shower can be social triggers. Even an innocent question from someone getting to know you, such as "Do you have kids/how many kids do you have?" can leave you confused and unsure about how to answer. *Should I mention my child from my miscarriage?* The very idea can be overwhelming and trigger a grief response.

I was out for dinner with a group of friends who were all parents with kids who happened to be a year or two apart. My daughter would have been one of the younger kids in the bunch at four years old, but she died of SIDS before her first birthday. Somehow, the group started discussing plans to take their kids on a road trip to an amusement park for little kids. All of us, including myself, were initially included in the conversation as we bounced ideas off each other; until one friend spoke up and said, "Oh, I didn't think you'd want to come, Jenna, because . . . you know." Immediately, all eyes shifted in my direction, and an uncomfortable silence fell over the table. At that moment, it hit me that I wasn't being included because I didn't meet the "parental" qualification.

My appetite was shot, and I ended up leaving the dinner early that day. Being caught off guard in that setting brought up emotions I didn't want to deal with in front of everyone.

—Jenna, 30

Verbal Triggers:

Sometimes people with good intentions say things to parents after a pregnancy or infant loss that are hurtful and may unintentionally trigger grief reactions such as sadness, anger, and frustration. The list below includes verbal triggers that those who contributed to this book have heard and how they made us feel.

What they said: *God needed another angel.*

How we felt: *God has plenty of angels; I needed my child.*

What they said: *God doesn't make mistakes.*

How we felt: *So you're saying God did this on purpose? That's cruel and doesn't make me feel good.*

What they said: *God had other plans.*

How we felt: *I wish those plans didn't include me losing my baby.*

What they said: *The baby just wasn't ready to be born yet.*

How we felt: *That doesn't make sense.*

What they said: *You can always have another baby.*

How we felt: *I wanted* this *baby. And the fact that I can have another baby doesn't mean I shouldn't feel sad about losing this one.*

What they said: *You can always adopt.*

How we felt: *That sounds like you want me to replace my lost baby with a new one.*

What they said: *You can always try again.*

How we felt: *Of course, I can, but that still won't replace this life that was lost.*

What they said: *You weren't ready for a baby anyway.*

How we felt: *It's not your place to say what I was ready for. Even if I wasn't ready, it was still my baby, and I didn't want to lose them.*

What they said: *It just wasn't meant to be.*

How we felt: *This isn't helpful in any way.*

What they said: *At least you weren't that far along in the pregnancy.*

How we felt: *Even if I was two seconds pregnant, this baby mattered to me.*

What they said: *At least you have other kids.*

How we felt: *That doesn't take away my pain over losing this one.*

What they said: *At least you know you can get pregnant.*

How we felt: *Getting pregnant doesn't replace the life lost. Also, getting pregnant again doesn't mean I won't have another loss.*

What they said: *They are in a better place now.*

How we felt: *There is no better place than here with me.*

What they said: *It wasn't a real baby.*

How we felt: *It was real to me.*

What they said: *It's not like you knew the baby.*

How we felt: *The baby was part of my body. I knew them in ways no one else did.*

What they said: *You probably should have done this/you should not have done that.*

How we felt: *It feels like you're blaming me for what happened, and I resent that.*

What they said: *You should have waited before telling people you were pregnant. You probably jinxed yourself.*

How we felt: *Blaming me through superstition is offensive and insulting.*

What they said: *Children are a lot of work; you aren't missing much.*

How we felt: *That's your opinion, one that minimizes my desire to be a parent.*

What they said: *You should be grateful for the great life you have.*

How we felt: *Being grateful for my life doesn't mean I don't deserve to grieve the loss of my child.*

What they said: *Now you can move on with your life.*

How we felt: *I will move on with my life, but I wish I could do it with my baby alive and well.*

What they said: *Think of it as a blessing in disguise.*

How we felt: *Losing something so precious is a tragedy, not a blessing.*

What they said: *Time heals all wounds.*

How we felt: *Some wounds don't heal with time; they get worse. It's going to take more than time to heal this pain.*

What they said: *It probably wouldn't have been healthy anyway.*

How we felt: *Even if they weren't healthy, they were still loved and valued by me.*

What they said: *I'm sure you'll have another one soon.*

How we felt: *You don't know that. Even if I have another baby soon, it doesn't replace this baby's life.*

What they said: *I know a person who had [x number of] miscarriages and still had a healthy baby; you'll be fine.*

How we felt: *Everyone's journey is different, and you have no way of knowing how things will turn out for me.*

What they said: *You're young; you can have more babies.*

How we felt: *I wanted this baby.*

What they said: *This happens to a lot of people; it's not a big deal.*

How we felt: *It's a big deal to me.*

What they said: *You should be over that by now.*

How we felt: *This isn't something you just "get over." You clearly don't value my baby the way I did, and I resent your lack of respect for my grief.*

What they said: *Maybe you should just get a pet.*

How we felt: *Maybe you should just stop talking.*

Responses to these comments can vary significantly among individuals. Words that comfort one person might be distressing to another. Creating and sharing a list of your verbal triggers with your loved ones may lead to more empathetic and supportive conversations. When loved ones are aware of what phrases may cause pain, they can consciously avoid them, reducing the likelihood of triggering a grief reaction. When creating your list, be open and honest about your feelings and include any phrases that have caused you pain in the past as well as those you fear might be hurtful. Feel free to use this list as guidance.

By recognizing the types of situations or circumstances that are likely to trigger a grief reaction, we can take steps to emotionally prepare ourselves for them and minimize their impact on us. The next section will show us how.

Navigating Grief Triggers

Dealing with grief triggers after a loss may feel like a never-ending challenge. But there are healthy ways you can regain control and tackle the triggers head-on.

Identify Telltale Physical Symptoms:

A good first step in navigating grief triggers is recognizing when something has triggered you. Some signs that can indicate a trigger may include crying, a racing pulse, sweating, feeling jitters, trembling, feeling hot or cold, nail-biting, bouncing knees, and pain such as a headache.

Acknowledge What You Are Feeling:

Being able to acknowledge when you are triggered requires honesty. Acknowledge the triggering moment and then take some time to reflect on the feelings it brings up, whether it's sadness over a memory, anger from an insensitive comment, envy that someone gets to enjoy time with their baby when you don't, or simply grief from longing. Acknowledging the root of what you feel will allow you to come to terms with it and use your coping skills to help get you through it. Revisit Chapters 4 and 5 for refreshers on "Coming to Terms" and "Coping Skills, Strategies, and Actions."

Create a Coping Plan:

You can create a plan to help you prepare for coping with expected and unexpected grief triggers.

Picture this: you're out shopping, going about your business, when suddenly a memory comes rushing back—one that triggers an emotional response. You feel your heart rate rise. Tears are already forming in the corners of your eyes. Panic starts to set in, and you can feel yourself losing control.

But wait. You remember the relaxation techniques you've been practicing for weeks. You find a quiet corner, close your eyes, and start to breathe. Inhale and exhale, deeply and slowly. You feel your body begin to relax as the tension fades away. You visualize a peaceful place where everything is calm and serene. You feel your mind and body slipping into this state of tranquility. When you open your eyes, you feel in control again.

Your coping plan should include relaxation techniques that can help you gain your composure in the moment and maintain your composure long-term. Regularly practicing techniques like deep breathing, meditation, or visualization can train your brain to automatically go to that calm place when you have a grief trigger. See Chapter 10 for more relaxation and mindfulness techniques.

When it comes to those anticipated grief triggers like holidays or anniversaries, it can be tempting to curl up in bed and avoid the world altogether. Instead, why not try creating new traditions that honor your loss in different, meaningful ways? You could set up a beautiful memorial space in your home with candles and flowers, something physical that will honor your baby in a way that uplifts you. This action plan is a great chance to reclaim your power over this recurring grief trigger. It serves double duty by honoring your baby and giving you an enriching way to express your grief. That said, your plan could very well be to stay in bed all day, curled up with a good book and some good food—and that's also okay. No matter what you choose, remember that your plan for navigating grief triggers should include coping in ways that make you feel most content.

There are additional strategies you can put in place to help you avoid potential triggers when returning to social settings:

<u>Communicate with your friends and loved ones ahead of time</u>. Set boundaries and tell them what you need. For example, you could say, "Hey guys, just a heads up, this is my first time going out since the loss happened. I'd rather not talk about it when we're out. Let's just enjoy each other's company and have a much-needed fun night out." Not only does this help you feel more comfortable, but it sets the tone for the outing and ensures everyone is on the same page.

<u>Excuse yourself from an event if you need to</u>. Events such as baby showers or holiday gatherings may be too emotionally overwhelming. Don't feel any pressure or obligation to attend. Do what feels right for you, whether that's skipping the event altogether or going and leaving early. Others may not fully understand at first, but they should come to respect your decision over time. Remember: taking care of yourself is not selfish. Allow yourself to focus on self-care and not worry about how people perceive your absence.

Talk It Out:

Coping with grief triggers can be easier when you have a support network. Whether it's sharing the facts of the situation that triggered your grief or simply venting your feelings, being able to communicate with someone you trust can be a lifeline when you're having a hard time.

Seek Professional ~~Help~~ Support:

If you find that you are struggling to recover from unexpected or recurrent grief triggers, seek professional support. A counselor or therapist can help you identify and plan for potential triggers, establish more effective coping mechanisms, and develop a personalized plan to work through your grief in a healthy and productive way. Revisit Chapter 8 for guidance on finding and building a good-fit relationship with your support professional.

Conclusion

The bottom line is this: by understanding the grief triggers you may encounter and having a plan to manage them, you'll be in a better position to cope with them in healthy ways.

Rest Stop

1. **Take a moment to reflect**. Write down a lesson from this chapter that will help guide your way, like creating a coping plan for expected and unexpected grief triggers.

2. **Take the *Crawl. Walk. Run. Soar.* self-assessment:**

   How are you feeling today? (circle one)

   Crawling – Making small but determined actions on your path to healing.

   Walking – Building momentum and making steady, consistent progress.

   Running – Taking rapid strides despite challenges.

   Soaring – Reaching new heights as you move forward toward an optimistic future.

   Remember: One day, you may soar, and the next, you may crawl. And that's okay. Healing isn't a linear journey with a set destination. It is continual progress toward feeling better.

3. **Take a break**. Give your mind a well-deserved break, then come back fresh and ready to dive into the next chapter tomorrow.

Notes

Chapter 10
Self-Care

Growing up, there wasn't much education around self-care. The most I heard of it was when people said "take care" as a salutation. After my pregnancy loss, I was advised to "take care of myself" without any real explanation of what that entailed. So, it was up to me to figure it out.

At first, I naively thought self-care meant bubble baths and face masks—which did nothing for me. Then I realized that it was more than just pampering; it's the action you take to help yourself recover physically, mentally, and emotionally, something I came to understand over time through reading books, having conversations with others, and trying new things.

Every day, I dedicated time toward caring for myself in whatever way felt right: journaling, meditating, or physical activity were just some of the activities I would do. And on days when I felt overwhelmed or unmotivated, doing one simple act to look after myself gave me something concrete to focus on and kept me moving forward with progress.

Now, when I come across someone going through grief or loss, instead of just telling them to "take care," I encourage them to practice self-care daily and give ideas on ways they can do it.

—Tawana, 39

How do you heal a wound? You care for it.

If you deeply cut your finger, you wouldn't just sit around and wait for time to heal it. You'd take action, cleaning it with water, then disinfecting it with peroxide and applying antibiotic ointment before covering it with a bandage. That's only the start. You would continue cleaning your finger and changing the dressing daily until the wound started feeling better and healing.

The same goes for self-care within the grief process. You are treating the pain of your loss by engaging in daily self-care activities to help you heal. To "heal" means to make whole again; it's the root of the word health. Tending to your health through self-care means putting in the much-needed effort to become whole again.

Let's be clear: being whole again doesn't mean returning to who you were before. We are forever changed by our experiences. But we can be whole in the sense that we can live a fulfilling life that brings us satisfaction and joy once again. Self-care is the key to getting there.

There are different ways to practice self-care, and in this chapter, we will discuss five types and how to incorporate them into our daily lives.

Five Types of Self-Care

Five major areas of our health can be affected after loss: emotional, mental, physical, social, and spiritual. To help us restore balance and work toward healing, let's explore each area and ways to practice self-care.

Emotional Health

Good emotional health revolves around our ability to manage and express the emotions that arise from our experiences. At its core, emotional health involves recognizing and understanding our feelings to self-regulate them so they don't overwhelm us. This means not suppressing difficult emotions but being aware of them and healthily processing them. When emotional health isn't nurtured, it can lead to problems such as irritability, anger, trouble sleeping, and even substance abuse. On the other hand, taking good care of our emotional health helps boost our overall well-being.

Interpreting our emotions is an essential part of maintaining emotional health. However, this can be easier said than done. Have you ever felt a certain way, and when someone asked what was wrong, you couldn't quite put it into words? This inability to articulate ourselves can create a barrier to understanding ourselves. Fortunately, there are tools available that can help make it easier, such as the Feeling Wheel created by Dr. Gloria Willcox. It's a tool for identifying, understanding, and expressing emotions. It consists of six basic categories of emotions: sad, mad, scared, joyful, powerful, and peaceful. Each of the categories contains several subcategories to help us gain a better understanding of what we are feeling.

When trying to identify and understand our emotions, we have to be honest with ourselves. We shouldn't focus on how we want to or should be feeling; instead, we should focus on how we do feel. Ask yourself, "What's preventing me from identifying this feeling?" "What thoughts am I thinking that could be contributing to my feelings?" "What do I need that would make me feel differently?" Writing down your answers can help you with brainstorming.

Once you've identified what emotion(s) you're experiencing, you must find healthy ways to express them. Some possible activities include writing in a journal; talking through it with a friend, family member, or therapist; engaging in creativity like painting or drawing; or getting outdoors for some fresh air. Doing any of these activities can help release pent-up emotions while allowing you the time and space to process them further.

We've created a three-step plan to make the process of emotional self-care a little easier:

1. Brainstorm how you feel, asking yourself prompt questions.

2. Identify the emotion(s) you are feeling using tools like the Feeling Wheel.

3. Find healthy ways to express your emotions with self-care activities like writing, talking it out, or creative activities.

Bonus step: Use a problem-focused coping strategy to channel your energy in a productive direction. (Revisit Chapter 5 for a refresher on Coping Skills, Strategies, and Actions.)

Let's look at a complete scenario:

After a loss, you're having lots of thoughts and emotions but don't know precisely what you are feeling. You do a brain dump and jot down your ideas on paper, asking yourself prompt questions to get closer to the answers. As you examine your notes and the Feeling Wheel, you determine that your primary feeling is *scared*. You aren't exactly sure what you're scared of, so you scan through the secondary emotions on the wheel and realize your fear is from feeling *helpless*.

It's not immediately clear what it is you feel helpless about. After some soul-searching, you realize it stems from the belief that you won't be able to conceive successfully in the future because of this loss. As you explore the outermost wheel, you see a word that sums it up for you: *discouraged*.

To healthily express your discouragement, you join an online loss support group, finding solace among a community of others who understand what you're going through. But the work doesn't have to stop there. Now it's time for your bonus step: problem-focused coping.

Having identified discouragement as the source of your fear and using self-care activities to express it, you then look for additional ways to combat this emotion. You decide to research your type of pregnancy loss at your local library. Your research reveals that, although common, most people with no other known issues who had a loss similar to yours will have successful pregnancies in the future. Now, rather than feeling discouraged, you feel more optimistic about your future, even hopeful.

Through honest reflection and analysis of your feelings, you're now on your way to feeling "whole" again. This is the power of emotional health and giving it the self-care it needs.

<u>Ways to Practice Emotional Self-Care</u>:

- Journal to reflect on your thoughts and feelings.
- Use tools like the Feeling Wheel to better understand and articulate your emotions.
- Engage in creative activities, like painting, writing, or dancing, to let your feelings flow freely.
- Use healthy coping strategies to manage difficult emotions and challenges in your life.

Mental Health

Mental health is more than just a buzzword. It's a broad and complex concept that refers to our overall psychological and emotional well-being. The state of our mental health determines our ability to think clearly, make good decisions, handle stress, and relate to other people. When our mental health isn't nurtured or maintained, it can seriously affect all aspects of our lives.

What's the difference between mental health and mental illness? These terms are often used interchangeably, but they refer to different things. Mental health refers to the state of your well-being. It encompasses many aspects, from emotional stability to cognitive abilities. On the other hand, mental illness is a diagnosable condition that meets specific criteria. While not everyone experiences a diagnosed mental illness, everyone's mental health is impacted at some point in life due to different factors, such as grief or a traumatic experience.

The grief of loss often brings with it a range of distressing emotions and anxiety. These feelings can be so intense that they disrupt daily life, leading to self-neglect and social withdrawal. People experiencing profound grief may have overwhelming emotional responses that further interfere with their mental well-being.

When our minds are overloaded due to grief, it can lead to mental exhaustion. This is why mental self-care is so necessary. Taking quick breaks throughout the day to sit in silence or take deep breaths can give our minds some much-needed relief.

But as technology advances and becomes more accessible, disconnecting from our screens is becoming increasingly difficult. Still, taking time away from our phones, computers, and TVs can positively impact our mental health. Research has shown that reducing screen time can help us concentrate better, increase our productivity, and even nurture relationships with the people around us. Taking the time to unplug and switch off devices also gives us the mental space to cope with our loss more effectively.

Sometimes you need a distraction to keep from focusing on the pain caused by your loss. Without screen time, where should you focus instead? Meditation can be the answer. Meditation is a practice that can bring deep relaxation and mental clarity. The basic process of meditation is simple: you focus on a single thought to bring calmness and free your mind from stress and external distractions.

Meditation can be done anywhere with no special equipment required. To begin meditating, find a comfortable place where you won't be disturbed or distracted. Sit or lie down with your eyes closed, then start taking deep breaths; think about nothing else but your breathing. Breathe in through your nose and out through your mouth for several minutes, allowing each breath to help you relax. As thoughts arise, acknowledge that they are there and focus back on your breathing: how many counts in, how many out, what it sounds like, what it feels like entering and leaving your lungs, etc.

Continue this pattern for however long it feels right; anywhere from ten to twenty minutes is often recommended. As you become more comfortable meditating, you may want to experiment with different postures, techniques, and mantras. Taking a group class is a great way to learn and connect with others. With regular practice, meditation can become another tool to combat feeling overwhelmed by grief.

> *I sat in my therapist's office, wondering if I had a mental illness. After losing our baby, I felt like a shell of myself. It was terrifying to experience such a loss of control. After an assessment, the therapist determined that while I didn't have a mental illness, I did have a tremendous amount of stress that was impacting my ability to cope. She suggested that I beef up my self-care to get me over the hump.*
>
> *Taking her advice, I began making small changes in my daily routine to better care for myself mentally. For example, instead of watching television or scrolling through social media at night, I took up reading—which I hadn't done in years and really enjoyed. During lunch breaks at work, instead of eating quickly at my desk, I read a book or took those few moments to close my eyes and be quiet and still, focusing on my breathing. Most helpful was giving myself permission to step away if things became too overwhelming or stressful at work or home.*
>
> *At first, it felt strange because I wasn't used to taking this kind of time out just for me. But now it feels like second nature, as necessary as brushing my teeth every day. It takes effort to keep it up, but it's definitely worth it. I'm finally feeling like me again.*
>
> —Dawn, 40

Guided imagery is a relaxation technique that can support mental health. It uses imagination to enter a deeply relaxed, meditative state. Start by finding a comfortable place to sit or lie down and close your eyes. Take several deep breaths and start imagining a peaceful, calming landscape; this can be somewhere you have been before or an entirely new imagined place. Explore this location in detail, focusing on the sights, sounds, and smells that come with it. As you continue exploring, concentrate on any positive emotions from being in this tranquil environment, such as contentment or peace. Focus on those emotions until the end of your practice session. Guided imagery can be done alone or with an audio recording, video, or live instructor. It's a nice go-to, especially in times of distress to help you regain peace.

The impact of self-care on mental health may seem small at first, but these moments of quality time with yourself can have tremendous benefits for your overall well-being.

Ways to Practice Mental Self-Care:

- Take breaks throughout the day to give your mind rest.
- Reduce screen time to get a break from unnecessary stimulation.
- Practice meditation or guided imagery to relax the body and mind.

Physical Health

When we are emotionally in pain, our physical body is also often taxed. To keep ourselves healthy when grieving, we have to take steps to ensure that our bodies function the best they can.

Building regular physical activity into our lives can help us stay motivated and energized while grieving. One way to do this is through exercise. Being regularly active has been shown to improve overall well-being by reducing stress levels and boosting moods by increasing brain endorphins (the "happy" hormones).

It probably sounds farfetched that you would suddenly become a gym rat in the middle of it all after a significant loss. That's not what we're suggesting. Instead, we are simply encouraging you to carve time out of your day to make room for some physical activity. From taking the dog out for an extra walk each day to taking the stairs instead of the elevator and even small actions like mobility exercises at home can make a significant difference in your body and in your ability to cope well during difficult times.

In addition to exercise, proper nutrition should be considered when dealing with grief and managing physical health. Eating nutrient-dense foods gives us essential vitamins and minerals that help the body maintain balance. When you're feeling down, eating a full meal might seem impossible, but that's where small but nutrient-dense snacks, like nuts and fruits, come in handy. And if you're still struggling to get all those necessary vitamins, multivitamins can help fill the gap. Avoiding unhealthy fats and sugars will help prevent extra strain on your system, and staying hydrated daily with plenty of water helps to keep your energy levels up.

Okay, we get it. Your eyes may be glazing over as you're wondering *how can eating healthier help me cope after losing my baby*? We know it doesn't seem like the two line up, but check this out. According to Harvard Medical School, the gut and the brain are connected. Researchers found that the gut may influence our emotions and cognitive capabilities. Studies also uncovered that nutritional strategies designed to support a healthy gut could soothe symptoms associated with grief. What does all this mean? Adding more nutritious foods like plants to our plates can help boost our emotional, mental, and physical health.

Herbs are a great way to add plants to our diet. They add flavor to dishes and offer other beneficial properties. For example:

- Parsley: lowers blood pressure
- Cinnamon: lowers blood sugar
- Chamomile: relaxes the nervous system
- Tulsi/holy basil: mood-boosting; reduces stress and anxiety

This is why herbal teas are so popular. They're not only tasty but also offer excellent physical benefits. So, when you're feeling especially run down, make that warm, soothing cup of tea, knowing that it is truly an act of self-care.

As a precaution, consult your doctor before trying new foods, supplements, or physical activities.

Finally, getting enough rest is necessary to caring for physical health. Rest is an essential part of a healthy lifestyle and helps to recharge our minds and bodies. Different types of rest can ensure we get the most out of our days.

Active Rest: Active rest involves low-intensity activities such as stretching, foam rolling, and leisurely walking. Not only does active rest help increase circulation in the body and reduce fatigue, but it can also improve mental clarity.

Passive Rest: Passive rest includes sleeping or relaxation time. Quality sleep helps support our immune system, gives us energy for daily tasks, and reduces stress hormone levels in the body to better cope with difficult emotions brought on by grief. Setting a bedtime routine with a consistent sleep schedule can help us maintain discipline. Additionally, allowing ourselves some downtime during the day, even fifteen minutes, can help reduce stress levels. (A nap in the car on your lunch break, anyone?)

Caring for your physical health can be invaluable when coping with loss. It allows us to find comfort in our bodies while providing stability when everything else feels chaotic and out of control. By engaging in activities such as exercise, following a nutritious diet, and getting adequate restful sleep, we create an empowering strategy that helps to build strength and endurance.

<u>Ways to Practice Physical Self-Care</u>:
- Eat well to help your body function at its best.

- Go to bed and wake up at the same time each day to help regulate your body's natural sleep rhythm.
- Exercise to help reduce stress levels.
- Take active rest to get your blood flowing and improve mental clarity.

Social Health

Social health is a leading factor in overall well-being. It can be defined as the degree to which a person feels socially connected, secure, and accepted within their environment. Social health can suffer without proper care and attention, leading to feelings of isolation, anxiety, and depression.

Chapter 8 covered "Defining Your Circle of Support" and ways to lean on them. One way to improve social health while coping with grief is through regular interaction with others. This helps create meaningful relationships and build a social support network. Another way to form a support network is to join a support group. The magic of a support group is that it allows people to give and receive support by sharing their experiences.

Volunteering is another excellent way to support social health when grieving a loss. It offers several important benefits, including posing a distraction and focusing on something positive, reminding us that we still have something valuable to offer, providing an outlet for our feelings, and boosting self-esteem by helping someone who is going through the same thing. Community organizations like Remembering Cherubs that support those facing pregnancy or infant loss can be great places to contribute your time and energy.

> *The depth of my grief made me feel like no one could possibly understand it. Things changed when I stumbled upon a booth at a health fair at my job. A non-profit group was handing out pamphlets about their mission and resources for grieving families. After talking to someone from the organization, they gave me an*

application to become a volunteer, saying that people who had gone through this experience make the best volunteers because they genuinely understand the value of the work. They explained how it could benefit me and others and offered their support every step of the way.

Through volunteering, I finally found people who understood what I was going through. It became a place where I fit in, giving me purpose and direction again. It also opened doors for personal growth by teaching me new skills, allowing me to take on new roles, and helping me learn more about a community I may not have become involved with had I not had a loss of my own. I'm so glad I committed to making a change that day. It's been an incredible journey ever since.

—Angel, 35

While volunteering has its benefits, there's no need to rush into this role. We should first ensure that we are emotionally and physically ready to take on such a responsibility. When the time comes, it can be a mutually rewarding experience for you and those in the organization you will serve.

It's clear that social health plays a significant role in overall well-being and shouldn't be overlooked when considering strategies for coping with grief. By being mindful of our needs, we can create healthier relationships that increase feelings of acceptance, belonging, and support.

Ways to Practice Social Self-Care:

- Create meaningful relationships to reduce feeling isolated.
- Define your circle of support to lean on them.
- Join a support group to give and receive support.
- Volunteer with a community organization to focus on and be a part of something positive.

Spiritual Health

Spirituality is often seen as a broad term that encompasses many different aspects of life. It generally refers to connecting with something beyond ourselves and can include religion, faith, and other beliefs. Religion is a set of practices, beliefs, and rituals that are shared within a particular society or culture. Faith is often regarded as the trust or belief in something without the need for proof or evidence.

Religions tend to be organized around specific doctrine, scriptures, and rituals which have been established by spiritual leaders. Generally speaking, all members of a particular religion share these basic tenets and practices that are believed to be sacred. Examples of religions include Buddhism, Christianity, Hinduism, Islam, and Judaism.

On the other hand, faith doesn't require any doctrine or specific beliefs to be held to practice it; instead, it's the trust or confidence in something without needing proof or evidence. An example of someone demonstrating faith could be believing in your inner strength and potential, even when the cards are stacked against you, or trusting a person and their abilities to handle a challenge.

At its core, spiritual health is a state of balance between the beliefs that help us lead a life filled with meaning and purpose.

After loss, many people turn to their spiritual beliefs for solace and a sense of purpose. Seeking meaning in a situation that feels unbearable can be incredibly beneficial. But when your beliefs clash with the reality of what you're going through, it can be a source of distress.

> *When the doctor said there was no heartbeat, my heart stopped too. I was in shock, unable to fully accept what was happening. One thought kept popping up in my mind between moments of gut-wrenching grief: How could something like this happen? That's when I began to feel angry at God; if He is truly loving and kind*

like everyone says, why would He take away something so precious from me? No amount of prayer seemed able to console this deep sense of betrayal I felt toward him.

—Michaela, 38

We must remember: our beliefs don't guarantee that we will be protected from pain and tragedy; unfortunately, suffering is part of the human experience.

Sometimes, a loss can send people into a spiritual crisis, leaving them disconnected from their beliefs. Reconnecting may seem like an impossible task. However, there are steps we can take to reestablish that connection.

Spiritual reconnection:

Spend time in nature. Nature provides an opportunity to reflect on the larger scheme of life itself and find appreciation in the world around you. Connecting with the natural world can bring us peace, harmony, and a sensation of connectedness to something greater. Immersing ourselves in nature also allows us to feel grounded and connected to the earth, recharging our spirit and allowing us to find balance in our lives.

Religious connection:

Attend religious services to engage with your community and focus on the higher power you believe in. Singing or praying with people of similar beliefs can reaffirm the unity of your community and create an atmosphere of connection. This allows you to strengthen your spiritual practice and deepen your relationships with those around you.

Faith reconnection:

Listen to uplifting stories online, on television, or even from people you know. Hearing about acts of kindness, courage, and selflessness can help remind you to have faith again.

When we live our lives in alignment with our beliefs and make time for activities that bring us peace, we can strengthen our spiritual health. This foundation can be an invaluable source to draw from as we cope with loss.

Ways to Practice Spiritual Self-Care:

- Connect with what you believe in to find fulfillment.
- Spend time outdoors to find peace and connect to the natural environment.
- Engage with your religious community to strengthen your practice.
- Look for the good in the world to help reinforce your faith.

Conclusion

The importance of self-care when coping with loss cannot be overstated. Taking care of all five aspects of ourselves—emotionally, mentally, physically, socially, and spiritually—gives us the power to lead an overall better quality of life and gets us closer to feeling whole again.

Rest Stop

1. **Take a moment to reflect.** Write down a lesson from this chapter that will help guide your way, like disconnecting from screens and intentionally engaging in self-care activities.
2. **Try practicing meditation or guided imagery.** Search online for local group classes or instructional videos.
3. **Take the *Crawl. Walk. Run. Soar.* self-assessment:**

    How are you feeling today? (circle one)

Crawling – Making small but determined actions on your path to healing.

Walking – Building momentum and making steady, consistent progress.

Running – Taking rapid strides despite challenges.

Soaring – Reaching new heights as you move forward toward an optimistic future.

Remember: One day, you may soar, and the next, you may crawl. And that's okay. Healing isn't a linear journey with a set destination. It is continual progress toward feeling better.

4. **Take a break**. Give your mind a well-deserved break, then come back fresh and ready to dive into the next chapter tomorrow.

Notes

Chapter 11
Goal-Setting

Setting goals is a practical tool for coping with grief after a pregnancy or infant loss. Let's look at the benefits of goal-setting and how it can support the coping techniques you've learned in this guidebook—plus using a vision board to help you stay focused.

Benefits of Goal-Setting

Navigating grief is like trying to find your way through an unfamiliar city without a map. It's disorienting, confusing, and easy to feel lost. That's where goal-setting comes in. Goal-setting means envisioning your ideal future and taking action to turn this vision into reality. Think of it as your GPS through the winding streets of grief. It won't make the road less bumpy, but it does provide a path forward.

Goal-setting offers numerous benefits:

- It helps us focus on what's most important to us.
- It allows us to create a sense of purpose in our lives.
- It improves self-confidence as we see progress toward our goals.
- It guides our choices on days when we aren't thinking clearly.
- It creates a sense of accomplishment and fulfillment.

Goal-setting can be rewarding, but only if the goals are reachable. Setting realistic goals improves our chances of seeing them through. Trying to do too much too soon can make us feel frustrated and disappointed.

For example:

Angel had a miscarriage at sixteen weeks. Immediately after her loss, she set a goal to be fully healed and emotionally ready to try for another pregnancy within one month. She believed this timeline would give her enough space to grieve, process her emotions, and fully move forward.

Despite her best efforts, Angel couldn't reach her goal within the one-month timeframe. Although she had made progress in her healing, she still had frequent bouts of unexpected grief and sadness that made her rethink growing her family so soon. She needed more time.

Healing from pregnancy or infant loss looks different from person to person. It doesn't happen on a set schedule and neither does conceiving another baby. While Angel's desire to be healed and conceive again was understandable, putting a deadline on grief or readiness is often a setup for a letdown.

It's best to start small, set goals we can actually reach, and build momentum over time with consistent effort.

"Without commitment, you'll never start. But more importantly, without consistency, you'll never finish."

—Denzel Washington

Here is a list of ideas to inspire forward progress on your goal-setting:

- Schedule a follow-up appointment with your doctor to ask questions and get a physical check-up.
- Decide on a meaningful way you'd like to memorialize your baby; choose memory-making activities you would feel most comforted by.

- Identify which healthy coping skills, strategies, and actions you resonate with the most and build a habit of referring to them.
- Create a plan for what you will do with the nursery, baby gifts, and other items, and see it through when you're ready.
- Determine whether you want to share the news of your loss. Then create a plan for who you will share the news with and how you will communicate it.
- Create a list of your support network, identify ways they can support you, and communicate your ideas with them when the time comes.
- Search for a counselor or therapist and follow the guidance in Chapter 8 to build a good-fit relationship with them.
- Make a coping plan to help you prepare for expected and unexpected grief triggers.
- Make a list of ways you can practice self-care. Each day, set a goal to do one of the self-care activities before the day ends.

Achieving Goals with a Vision Board

If you want to bring your goals to life, consider creating a vision board.

A vision board is simply a visual representation of your goals. It's typically created with cut-outs of specific images, words, pictures, and even colors that symbolize what you want to accomplish. The images can be cut from magazines, printed online, or even hand-drawn. Words can range from inspirational quotes to affirmations or even specific goals written out in detail.

Vision boards are excellent tools for helping us stay focused on our goals and clarifying where we want to go in life. It's like taking puzzle pieces out of a box and organizing them to create a clear picture. The idea is to look at it daily to keep our goals at the forefront of our minds.

Before diving into the creative process for your vision board, take time to get clarity on what you want to manifest in your life. Start by asking yourself questions like "What do I want?", "What areas of my life need attention right now?", and "What do I want my future self to look like?" Asking these questions will help clarify what you want to accomplish so that it's clearly reflected when creating imagery for your vision board.

Once you've decided on your goals, start gathering materials for your vision board.

Suggested materials:

- A poster board or large cork board: something that has a stable background and makes it easy to move visual elements around.
- Glue sticks, tape, or other adhesives to attach the visuals onto the board.
- Images that reflect your goals: printed photos and cut-outs of words, images, and quotes. Avoid using images or words that are small or have a font that's hard to see and could easily be missed when looking at your board.
- Markers and colored pencils: these are handy for manually writing words or drawing images.
- Stickers or other embellishments: adding attention-grabbing stickers or decorative accents can give the vision board more character.

After identifying your goals and gathering your materials, you're ready to create your vision board. Start by laying out all the materials onto a large surface area (such as a tabletop or floor) for easy access. Don't use any glue, tape, or other adhesive just yet. We want to get the layout just right first before we seal them permanently in place.

Next, aim to arrange the various elements in a way that makes sense. For example, if your biggest goal is to get more sleep at night, you could have the images and words related to that goal be a significant focal point on your vision board by putting them directly in the center. Be creative; there isn't really a wrong way to do it. Experiment with arranging all the elements, grouping them together by a specific goal, color, size, or whatever way looks good to you.

Take time throughout the creation process to step back and see how it looks from different angles and continue with more additions/edits if necessary. Don't worry about trying to make it perfect or if you aren't the creative type. What matters most is that you can clearly see the images and read the words.

When you're satisfied with how everything looks, use your adhesives to attach each item securely onto the board. Finally, once everything is in place, decide where you want to hang up your vision board.

Here are some ideas:

Your bedroom or living room

Your bedroom or living room are great places to hang your vision board because you likely spend a lot of time there. Seeing your vision board each day will help keep your goals at the forefront of your mind and remind you of what you're working toward.

Your office

If you have an office or work space, hanging your vision board there can inspire and motivate you throughout the workday. It's a great way to stay focused on your goals and stay positive when things get tough.

Anywhere else that inspires you

There are no rules about where you have to hang your vision board. If there's somewhere else that inspires you, go for it. Maybe it's in your kitchen, so you see it every time you make dinner, or maybe it's in your bathroom, so you see it every time you get ready for the day. Wherever it is, make sure it's somewhere you'll actually be able to see and be inspired by it.

Here is a sample board we created and how we came up with it:

We first started by identifying our goals. We centered ours around five main areas of our health:

Emotional goal:

Use the Feeling Wheel when I struggle to identify or express my emotions.

Mental goal:

Learn how to meditate and set aside time every day to practice it.

Physical goal:

Eat well to help my body function at its best capacity.

Social goal:

Volunteer with a community organization.

Spiritual goal:

Look for the good in each day to rebuild my faith.

Then we wrote down coping skills, strategies, and actions we want to get better at:

- Protect my peace
- Ask for help when I need it
- Write in my notebook
- Include more plants on my plate

Combining images, phrases, and our goals, we were able to create a visual representation of what we wanted to be reminded of each day.

Looking through our list of goals and the things we want to improve, you'll see that it's all represented here on our board. It's not fancy or the best-looking board in the world. But it gets the job done.

Creating a vision board helps us manifest our goals into reality by clarifying our intentions and keeping us motivated. Progress doesn't happen overnight. But staying focused and applying consistent daily effort will eventually show results—so stick with it.

Conclusion

Setting and reaching goals that support our healing can be a powerful way of addressing the complex challenges we face after losing a pregnancy or infant. At the end of the day, we should set realistic expectations and celebrate progress, no matter how small it may seem. Making a vision board and looking at it every day can help us stay motivated and focused. Although progress isn't always easy, dedicating consistent effort will eventually get us closer to where we're headed.

Rest Stop

1. **Take a moment to reflect**. Write down a lesson from this chapter that will help guide your way, like setting realistic, achievable goals.

2. **Write out your goals and build a vision board around them.**

3. **Take the *Crawl. Walk. Run. Soar.* self-assessment:**

    How are you feeling today? (circle one)

    Crawling – Making small but determined actions on your path to healing.

    Walking – Building momentum and making steady, consistent progress.

    Running – Taking rapid strides despite challenges.

    Soaring – Reaching new heights as you move forward toward an optimistic future.

    Remember: One day, you may soar, and the next, you may crawl. And that's okay. Healing isn't a linear journey with a set destination. It is continual progress toward feeling better.

4. **Take a break**. Give your mind a well-deserved break, then come back fresh and ready to dive into the conclusion chapter tomorrow!

Notes

Conclusion

So, where do we go from here? We go forward. In the wake of losing a pregnancy or infant, one of the most impactful things we can do is equip ourselves with the tools of knowledge and guidance to cope well and forge our way forward on a path toward healing.

In this guidebook, we have provided comprehensive information to help you navigate your continued journey.

We began by exploring the administrative aspects of loss, including reporting requirements, memorialization options, and common causes of loss—which we now know are mostly beyond our control. Our hope is that this information will help alleviate some of the burdens of navigating this process uninformed.

We then examined the unique challenges parents face and also highlighted the physical experiences of loss, ways to accept a complicated reality, and strategies for coping with grief.

Next, we covered the importance of support for partners and precise ways to communicate our news with adults and children.

Finally, we explored life after loss, including accepting support, navigating triggers, and best practices for self-care. We hope this gave you some insight into restoring your peace of mind.

We understand that everyone's path through pregnancy and infant loss is unique. Still, we have faith that this guidebook can be a source that speaks to circumstances you will encounter. It's designed to be a lifelong companion you can turn to time and again. It's not meant to be read once and then shelved; it's a living, breathing resource that will continue to offer value each time you revisit its pages, evolving with you as you grow and change. So, keep it close. Revisit it often. Let it serve as a constant source of support, encouragement, and guidance on your path.

Remember to be patient with yourself, seek support when needed, and take it one day at a time. You are stronger than you know and will come out the other side.

I hope you found the information provided in this guidebook to be helpful. I'm always looking for ways to improve our resources and better serve the pregnancy and infant loss community.

That's why I'm asking for your feedback. Please take a moment to complete a short satisfaction survey by visiting the following link:

www.rememberingcherubs.org/guidebook-survey

Your responses will help me understand what was done well and where improvements can be made in future editions of this guidebook. Thank you for your time and input.

—Monica Sholar Anderson

Monica Sholar Anderson is a nationally certified community health worker and the proud founder and executive director of Remembering Cherubs, a non-profit organization that provides support services for bereaved parents facing pregnancy and infant loss.

In addition to her work with Remembering Cherubs, Monica serves on the Perinatal Infant Reproductive Loss (PIRL) Committee for the University of Michigan Health System. In this role, she works closely with healthcare professionals to ensure that the best medical practices are implemented for those dealing with such losses. She is also a Fetal Infant Mortality Review (FIMR) Taskforce member with the Detroit Health Department.

Through her various roles, Monica tirelessly advocates for parents suffering from grief and loss, creating avenues to provide them with the essential support resources they deserve.

To learn more, visit: www.rememberingcherubs.org

Bibliography

Chapter One:

- Agency for Healthcare Research and Quality. (Last reviewed, September 2020). *Follow-Up with Patients: Tool #6*. Retrieved 2023, from https://www.ahrq.gov/health-literacy/improve/precautions/tool6.html#:~:text=Overview,further%20assessments%20and%20adjust%20treatments

- American College of Obstetricians and Gynecologists. (n.d.). *Early Pregnancy Loss*. Retrieved 2023, from https://www.acog.org/womens-health/faqs/early-pregnancy-loss

- Centers for Disease Control and Prevention. (2020). *User Guide to the 2020 Fetal Death Public Use File*. Retrieved 2023, from https://ftp.cdc.gov/pub/Health_Statistics/NCHS/Dataset_Documentation/DVS/fetaldeath/2020fetaluserguide.pdf

- Centers for Disease Control and Prevention. (Last reviewed, April 11, 2016). *Mortality Records with Mention of International Classification of Diseases-10 code P96.4 (Termination of Pregnancy): United States, 2003–2014.* Retrieved 2023, from https://www.cdc.gov/nchs/health_policy/mortality-records-mentioning-termination-of-pregnancy.htm

- Centers for Disease Control and Prevention. (Last reviewed, November 19, 2020). *Surveillance of Congenital Anomalies*. Retrieved 2023, from https://www.cdc.gov/ncbddd/

- birthdefects/surveillancemanual/chapters/chapter-1/chapter1-4.html#:~:text=These%20are%20defined%20as%20structural,cleft%20lip%20and%20spina%20bifida.

- Centers for Disease Control and Prevention. (Last reviewed, November 17, 2022). *CDCs Abortion Surveillance System FAQs*. Retrieved 2023, from https://www.cdc.gov/reproductivehealth/data_stats/abortion.htm

- Centers for Disease Control and Prevention. (Last reviewed, September 29, 2022). *What Is Stillbirth*. Retrieved 2023, from https://www.cdc.gov/ncbddd/stillbirth/facts.html#:~:text=Stillbirth%20affects%20about%201%20in,stillborn%20in%20the%20United%20States.&text=That%20is%20about%20the%20same,the%20first%20year%20of%20life

- Centers for Disease Control and Prevention/National Center for Health Statistics. (1997). *State Definitions and Reporting Requirements for Live Births, Fetal Deaths, and Induced Terminations of Pregnancy*. Retrieved 2023, from https://www.cdc.gov/nchs/data/misc/itop97.pdf

- Cornell Health. (n.d.). *Study Breaks & Stress Busters*. Retrieved 2023, from https://health.cornell.edu/about/news/study-breaks-stress-busters#:~:text=Research%20shows%20that%20taking%20purposeful,productivity%2C%20and%20ability%20to%20focus

- Danielsson, K. (2022). *What Is Fetal Viability?* Retrieved 2023, from https://www.verywellfamily.com/premature-birth-and-viability-2371529

- Donate Life America. (n.d.). *Tissue Donation*. Retrieved 2023, from https://donatelife.net/donation/organs/tissue-donation/

- Gift of Life Michigan. (n.d.). *About Donation*. Retrieved 2023, from https://giftoflifemichigan.org/about-donation

- Guttmacher Institute. (As of July 1, 2023). *Abortion Reporting Requirements.* Retrieved 2023, from https://www.guttmacher.org/state-policy/explore/abortion-reporting-requirements

- Guttmacher Institute. (As of July 1, 2023). *State Bans on Abortion throughout Pregnancy.* Retrieved 2023, from https://www.guttmacher.org/state-policy/explore/state-policies-later-abortions

- Intermountain Healthcare. (n.d.). *Miscarriage before 20 weeks: Options for Care of Fetal Remains.* Retrieved 2023, from https://intermountainhealthcare.org/ckr-ext/Dcmnt?ncid=529806023

- Mansell, A. (2006). *Early Pregnancy Loss.* Emergency Nurse.

- Michigan Legislature. (n.d.). *House Legislative Analysis.* Analysis as Passed by the House. Retrieved 2023, from http://www.legislature.mi.gov/documents/2011-2012/billanalysis/House/htm/2011-HLA-5711-3.htm

- Natera. (n.d.). *Instructions for At-Home Collection of Miscarriage Tissue.* Retrieved 2023, from https://www.natera.com/wp-content/uploads/2021/02/Womens-Health-Patient-Anora-Instructions-for-At-Home-Collection-of-Miscarriage-Tissue.pdf

- National Center for Health Statistics. (Last reviewed, November 6, 2015). *State Definitions and Reporting Requirements for Live Births, Fetal Deaths, and Induced Terminations of Pregnancy.* Retrieved 2023, from https://www.cdc.gov/nchs/products/other/miscpub/statereq.htm

- National Center for Health Statistics. (Last reviewed, October 18, 2022). *NVSS – Fetal Deaths.* Retrieved 2023, from https://www.cdc.gov/nchs/nvss/fetal_death.htm

- PainScale. (n.d.). *6 Tips for Communicating during Doctor Appointments.* Retrieved 2023, from https://www.painscale.com/article/6-tips-for-communicating-during-doctor-appointments

- Remembering Our Babies. (n.d.). *Pregnancy and Infant Loss Remembrance Day*. Retrieved 2023, from https://www.october15th.com/

- State of Michigan. (2022). *October 2022: Pregnancy and Infant Loss Awareness Month*. Retrieved 2023, from https://www.michigan.gov/whitmer/news/proclamations/2022/10/15/october-2022-pregnancy-and-infant-loss-awareness-month

- The United States Conference of Catholic Bishops. (n.d.). *Care of Fetal Remains*. Retrieved 2023, from https://files.ecatholic.com/23075/documents/2019/11/Care%20of%20Fetal%20Remains.pdf?t=1574875059000

- University of Michigan Women's Health. (n.d.). *Financial and Legal Concerns after Pregnancy Loss*. Retrieved 2023, from https://www.umwomenshealth.org/resources/pregnancy-loss-financial-legal-concerns

- Weigel, et al. (2019). *Understanding Pregnancy Loss in the Context of Abortion Restrictions and Fetal Harm Laws*. KFF. Retrieved 2023, from https://www.kff.org/womens-health-policy/issue-brief/understanding-pregnancy-loss-in-the-context-of-abortion-restrictions-and-fetal-harm-laws/

Chapter Two:

- American College of Obstetricians and Gynecologists. (2019, September 25). *Abortion Can Be Medically Necessary*. Retrieved 2023, from https://www.acog.org/news/news-releases/2019/09/abortion-can-be-medically-necessary

- American College of Obstetricians and Gynecologists. (2022, August 15). *Understanding and Navigating Medical Emergency Exceptions In Abortion Bans and Restrictions*. Retrieved 2023,

- from https://www.acog.org/news/news-articles/2022/08/understanding-medical-emergency-exceptions-in-abortion-bans-restrictions

- American Diabetes Association. (Updated 2022, September 14). *Signs of Miscarriage*. Retrieved 2023, from https://ada.com/signs-of-miscarriage/

- Berend Z. Surrogate Losses: *Understandings of Pregnancy Loss and Assisted Reproduction among Surrogate Mothers*. Med Anthropol Q. 2010 Jun; 24(2):240–62. doi: 10.1111/j.1548-1387.2010.01099.x. PMID: 20550095.

- Bryant, H. (2008). *Maintaining Patient Dignity and Offering Support after Miscarriage.* Emergency Nurse.

- Centers for Disease Control and Prevention. (n.d.). *About SUID and SIDS*. Retrieved 2023, from https://www.cdc.gov/sids/about/index.htm

- Centers for Disease Control and Prevention. (n.d.). *Basic Information about Uterine Cancer*. Retrieved 2023, from https://www.cdc.gov/cancer/uterine/basic_info/index.htm#:~:text=The%20uterus%20is%20the%20pear,your%20uterus%2C%20called%20the%20endometrium.

- Centers for Disease Control and Prevention. (n.d.). *Congenital Anomalies—Definitions*. Retrieved 2023, from https://www.cdc.gov/ncbddd/birthdefects/surveillancemanual/chapters/chapter-1/chapter1-4.html#:~:text=These%20are%20defined%20as%20structural,cleft%20lip%20and%20spina%20bifida.

- Centers for Disease Control and Prevention. (n.d.). *Infant Mortality*. Retrieved 2023, from https://www.cdc.gov/reproductivehealth/maternalinfanthealth/infantmortality.htm

- Centers for Disease Control and Prevention. (n.d.). *Infertility FAQs*. Retrieved 2023, from https://www.cdc.gov/reproductivehealth/infertility/index.htm

- Centers for Disease Control and Prevention. (n.d.). *Injuries among Children and Teens*. Retrieved 2023, from https://www.cdc.gov/injury/features/child-injury/index.html

- Centers for Disease Control and Prevention. (n.d.). *What Is Stillbirth*. Retrieved 2023, from https://www.cdc.gov/ncbddd/stillbirth/facts.html

- Centers for Disease Control and Prevention/National Center for Health Statistics. (1997). *State Definitions and Reporting Requirements for Live Births, Fetal Deaths, and Induced Terminations of Pregnancy*. Retrieved 2023, from https://www.cdc.gov/nchs/data/misc/itop97.pdf

- Cleveland Clinic. (n.d.). *Chemical Pregnancy*. Retrieved 2023, from https://my.clevelandclinic.org/health/diseases/22188-chemical-pregnancy#:~:text=What%20is%20a%20chemical%20pregnancy,miscarry%20don't%20realize%20it.

- Cleveland Clinic. (n.d.). *Fetal Development*. Retrieved 2023, from https://my.clevelandclinic.org/health/articles/7247-fetal-development-stages-of-growth#:~:text=Generally%2C%20it's%20called%20an%20embryo,a%20fetus%20until%20it's%20born.

- Cleveland Clinic. (n.d.). *Medical Abortion*. Retrieved 2023, from https://my.clevelandclinic.org/health/treatments/21899-medical-abortion

- Cleveland Clinic. (n.d.). *Stillbirth*. Retrieved 2023, from https://my.clevelandclinic.org/health/diseases/9685-stillbirth#:~:text=If%20your%20lifestyle%20includes%20drinking,the%20fetus%2C%20including%20an%20autopsy.

BIBLIOGRAPHY

- Cleveland Clinic. (n.d.). *Vanishing Twin Syndrome.* Retrieved 2023, from https://my.clevelandclinic.org/health/diseases/23023-vanishing-twin-syndrome

- Danielsson, K. (Updated 2021, September 13). *Different Types of Pregnancy Loss.* Verywell Family. Retrieved 2023, from https://www.verywellfamily.com/types-of-pregnancy-loss-2371413

- Evans, et al., (2023). *A Qualitative Exploration Of Stressors: Voices of African American Women Who Have Experienced Each Type of Fetal/Infant Loss: Miscarriage, Stillbirth, and Infant Mortality.* Journal of Black Psychology, 49(2), 236–263. https://doi.org/10.1177/00957984221112833

- EveryDay Health (n.d.). *6 Scenarios Where Abortion Can Be Lifesaving.* Retrieved 2023, from https://www.everydayhealth.com/abortion/scenarios-where-abortion-can-be-life-saving/

- GYN Choices of Central Jersey. (n.d.). *Understanding the Difference between a Medical and Surgical Abortion.* Retrieved 2023, from https://www.gynchoicesofcentraljersey.com/blog/understanding-the-difference-between-a-medical-and-surgical-abortion/

- Gyn Choices of Central New Jersey. *Understanding the Difference between a Medical and Surgical Abortion.* Retrieved 2023, from https://www.gynchoicesofcentraljersey.com/blog/understanding-the-difference-between-a-medical-and-surgical-abortion/

- Heinke D., Nestoridi E., Hernandez-Diaz S., Williams P.L., Rich-Edwards J.W., Lin A.E., Van Bennekom C.M., Mitchell A.A., Nembhard W.N., Fretts R.C., Roberts D.J., Duke C.W., Carmichael S.L., Yazdy M.M.; *National Birth Defects Prevention Study. Risk of Stillbirth for Fetuses with Specific Birth Defects.* Obstet Gynecol.

- 2020 Jan; 135(1):133–140. doi: 10.1097/AOG.0000000000003614. PMID: 31809437; PMCID: PMC7033649.

- Horsager-Boehrer, R. (2018). *What Happens if the Umbilical Cord Is around My Baby's Neck?* UT Southwestern Medical Center. Retrieved 2023, from https://utswmed.org/medblog/nuchal-cord-during-pregnancy/#:~:text=When%20is%20a%20nuchal%20cord,off%2C%20a%20stillbirth%20can%20occur.

- Kaiser Family Foundation. (n.d.). *Abortion Gestational Limits and Exceptions*. Retrieved 2023 from https://www.kff.org/womens-health-policy/state-indicator/gestational-limit-abortions/?currentTimeframe=0&sortModel=%7B%22colId%22:%22Location%22,%22sort%22:%22asc%22%7D

- Leon, I.G., (2010). *Understanding and Treating Infertility: Psychoanalytic Considerations.* Journal of the American Academy of Psychoanalysis and Dynamic Psychiatry, 38(1) 47–75, 2010.

- Leon, I.G., (2017). *Empathic Psychotherapy for Pregnancy Termination for Fetal Anomaly.* Psychotherapy Vol. 54, No. 4, 394–399.

- March of Dimes. (2021, November 2). *March Of Dimes Kicks Off Prematurity Awareness Month with New PSA Highlighting Families Impacted by Maternal & Infant Health Issues.* Retrieved 2023, from https://www.marchofdimes.org/about/news/march-dimes-kicks-prematurity-awareness-month-new-psa-highlighting-families-impacted#:~:text=As%20many%20as%20half%20of,CEO%20of%20March%20of%20Dimes.

- March of Dimes. (n.d.). *Low Birthweight.* Retrieved 2023, from https://www.marchofdimes.org/find-support/topics/birth/low-birthweight

- March of Dimes. (n.d.). *Miscarriage*. Retrieved 2023, from https://www.marchofdimes.org/find-support/topics/miscarriage-loss-grief/miscarriage
- March of Dimes. (n.d.). *Preterm Labor and Premature Birth: Are You at Risk?* Retrieved 2023, from https://www.marchofdimes.org/find-support/topics/birth/preterm-labor-and-premature-birth-are-you-risk
- Mayo Clinic. (n.d.). *Blighted Ovum: What Causes It?* Retrieved 2023, from https://www.mayoclinic.org/diseases-conditions/pregnancy-loss-miscarriage/expert-answers/blighted-ovum/faq-20057783
- Mayo Clinic. (n.d.). *Ectopic Pregnancy*. Retrieved 2023, from https://www.mayoclinic.org/diseases-conditions/ectopic-pregnancy/symptoms-causes/syc-20372088#:~:text=An%20ectopic%20pregnancy%20can't,threatening%20bleeding%2C%20if%20left%20untreated.
- Mayo Clinic. (n.d.). *Fetal Development: The 1st Trimester*. Retrieved 2023, from https://www.mayoclinic.org/healthy-lifestyle/pregnancy-week-by-week/in-depth/prenatal-care/art-20045302
- Mayo Clinic. (n.d.). *In Vitro Fertilization (IVF)*. Retrieved 2023, from https://www.mayoclinic.org/tests-procedures/in-vitro-fertilization/about/pac-20384716
- Mayo Clinic. (n.d.). *Miscarriage*. Retrieved 2023, from https://www.mayoclinic.org/diseases-conditions/pregnancy-loss-miscarriage/diagnosis-treatment/drc-20354304#:~:text=In%20a%20missed%20miscarriage%2C%20the,miscarriages%20occurring%20before%2012%20weeks.

- Mayo Clinic. (n.d.). *Preeclampsia*. Retrieved 2023, from https://www.mayoclinic.org/diseases-conditions/preeclampsia/symptoms-causes/syc-20355745

- Mayo Clinic. (n.d.). *Sudden Infant Death Syndrome (SIDS)*. Retrieved 2023, from https://www.mayoclinic.org/diseases-conditions/sudden-infant-death-syndrome/symptoms-causes/syc-20352800

- Mayo Clinic. (n.d.). *The Placenta: How It Works, What's Normal*. Retrieved 2023, from https://www.mayoclinic.org/healthy-lifestyle/pregnancy-week-by-week/in-depth/placenta/art-20044425#:~:text=The%20placenta%20is%20an%20organ,umbilical%20cord%20arises%20from%20it.

- National Library of Medicine. (n.d.). *Gestational Age*. Retrieved 2023, from https://medlineplus.gov/ency/article/002367.htm#:~:text=Gestation%20is%20the%20period%20of,far%20along%20the%20pregnancy%20is.

- National Library of Medicine. (n.d.). *Miscarriage*. Retrieved 2023, from https://medlineplus.gov/ency/article/001488.htm

- NCH Healthcare System. (n.d.). *Miscarriage*. Retrieved 2023, from https://nchmd.org/health-library/diseases-and-conditions/con-20198833/

- NHS. (n.d.) *Stillbirth*. Retrieved 2023, from https://www.nhs.uk/conditions/stillbirth/causes/

- Omar N., Major S., Mohsen M., Al Tamimi H., El Taher F., Kilshaw S. Culpability, Blame, and Stigma after Pregnancy Loss in Qatar. BMC Pregnancy Childbirth. 2019 Jun 26; 19(1):215. doi: 10.1186/s12884-019-2354-z. PMID: 31242874; PMCID: PMC6595691.

BIBLIOGRAPHY

- Peters, et al. (2014). *Measuring African American Women's Trust in Provider during Pregnancy*. Research In Nursing & Health

- Sobczak A., Taylor L., Solomon S., Ho J., Kemper S., Phillips B., Jacobson K., Castellano C., Ring A., Castellano B., Jacobs R.J.. *The Effect of Doulas on Maternal and Birth Outcomes: A Scoping Review*. Cureus. 2023 May 24; 15(5):e39451. doi: 10.7759/cureus.39451. PMID: 37378162; PMCID: PMC10292163.

- Stanford Medicine. (n.d.). *Overview of Pregnancy Loss*. Retrieved 2023, from https://www.stanfordchildrens.org/en/topic/default?id=overview-of-pregnancy-loss-90-P02466

- Tommy's. (n.d.). *Incomplete Miscarriage*. Retrieved 2023, from https://www.tommys.org/baby-loss-support/miscarriage-information-and-support/types-of-miscarriage/incomplete-miscarriage#:~:text=What%20is%20an%20incomplete%20miscarriage,tissue%20stays%20in%20the%20womb

- Turman J.E. Jr., and Swigonski N.L. (2021). *Changing Systems that Influence Birth Outcomes in Marginalized Zip Codes*. Pediatrics. Jul; 148(1):e2020049651. doi: 10.1542/peds.2020-049651. Epub 2021, Jun 2. PMID: 34078748.

Chapter Three:

- American Diabetes Association. (Updated 2022, September 14). *Signs of Miscarriage*. Retrieved 2023, from https://ada.com/signs-of-miscarriage/

- Baylor College of Medicine. (2018, March 2). *What Is a Parent? How Policy Shapes the Definition of Parenthood*. Retrieved 2023, from https://blogs.bcm.edu/2018/03/02/parent-policy-shapes-definition-parenthood/#:~:text=Gestational%20parent%3A%20

The%20individual%20who,responsibility%20for%20custody%20or%20support

- Baylor College of Medicine. (2018, March 2). *What Is a parent? How Policy Shapes the Definition of Parenthood*. Retrieved 2023, from https://blogs.bcm.edu/2018/03/02/parent-policy-shapes-definition-parenthood/#:~:text=Gestational%20parent%3A%20The%20individual%20who,responsibility%20for%20custody%20or%20support

- Big Think. (2019, August 26). *Can You Use Narrative to Shape Your Life?* Retrieved from https://bigthink.com/neuropsych/storytelling-narrative-psychology/

- Bullock, B. G. (2017). *How to Stop Your Stories from Running Your Life*. Mindful. Retrieved 2023, from https://www.mindful.org/stop-stories-running-life/

- Circle Surrogacy. (n.d.). *What Is Surrogacy?* Retrieved 2023, from https://www.circlesurrogacy.com/about/what-is-surrogacy

- Cleveland Clinic. (n.d.). *Chills*. Retrieved 2023, from https://my.clevelandclinic.org/health/symptoms/21476-chills

- Cleveland Clinic. (n.d.). *Lochia*. Retrieved 2023, from https://my.clevelandclinic.org/health/symptoms/22485-lochia#:~:text=Lochia%20alba%20is%20the%20last%20stage%20of%20lochia.&text=Yellowish%20white%20discharge.,12%20days%20to%20six%20weeks.

- Cleveland Clinic. (n.d.). *Miscarriage*. Retrieved 2023, from https://my.clevelandclinic.org/health/diseases/9688-miscarriage

- Danielsson, K. (Updated 2022, September 19). *How to Know If You're Hemorrhaging Due to a Miscarriage*. Verywell Family. Retrieved 2023, from https://www.verywellfamily.com/

- hemorrhage-in-miscarriage-meaning-2371523#:~:text=If%20you%20bleed%20through%20a,toilet%20bowl%20full%20of%20water

- Duffy, J. (2018). *Stress, Story, and the Unspoken Connection*. Psychology Today. Retrieved 2023, from https://www.psychologytoday.com/us/blog/the-power-personal-narrative/201810/stress-story-and-the-unspoken-connection

- Healthline. (n.d.). *After Abortion Care: What to Expect after Your Abortion*. Retrieved 2023, from https://www.healthline.com/health/after-abortion#complications

- Healthline. (n.d.). *What Causes Concurring Vomiting and Diarrhea, and How Is It Treated?* Retrieved 2023, from https://www.healthline.com/health/diarrhea-and-vomiting#treatment

- Healthline. (n.d.). *What Is a Rainbow Baby?* Retrieved 2023, from https://www.healthline.com/health/pregnancy/rainbow-baby

- Leon, I. G., (1999). Understanding Pregnancy Loss: Helping Families Cope. *Postgraduate Obstetrics & Gynecology.*

- Liverpool Women's NHS Foundation Trust. (n.d.). *Lactation after Loss*. Retrieved 2023, from https://liverpoolwomens.nhs.uk/media/3745/lactation-after-loss-leaflet.pdf

- March of Dimes. (n.d.). *Your Body after Baby: The First 6 Weeks*. Retrieved 2023, from https://www.marchofdimes.org/find-support/topics/postpartum/your-body-after-baby-first-6-weeks

- Mayo Clinic. (n.d.). *Breast Pain*. Retrieved 2023, from https://www.mayoclinic.org/diseases-conditions/breast-pain/symptoms-causes/syc-20350423

- Mayo Clinic. (n.d.). *Fever Treatment: Quick Guide to Treating a Fever*. Retrieved 2023, from https://www.mayoclinic.org/diseases-conditions/fever/in-depth/fever/art-20050997

- Mayo Clinic. (n.d.). *Fever: First Aid*. Retrieved 2023, from https://www.mayoclinic.org/first-aid/first-aid-fever/basics/art-20056685

- Mayo Clinic. (n.d.). *Hemorrhoids*. Retrieved 2023, from https://www.mayoclinic.org/diseases-conditions/hemorrhoids/diagnosis-treatment/drc-20360280#:~:text=Apply%20an%20over%2Dthe%2Dcounter,bath%20fits%20over%20the%20toilet

- Mayo Clinic. (n.d.). *Postpartum Care: What to Expect after a Vaginal Birth*. Retrieved 2023, from https://www.mayoclinic.org/healthy-lifestyle/labor-and-delivery/in-depth/postpartum-care/art-20047233

- Mayo Clinic. (n.d.). *Vaginal Bleeding*: Retrieved 2023, from https://www.mayoclinic.org/symptoms/vaginal-bleeding/basics/definition/sym-20050756

- Media Partners. (2018, August 6). *The Science of Storytelling: How Storytelling Shapes Our Behavior*. Retrieved 2023, from https://www.mediapartners.com/blog/post/the_science_of_storytelling_how_storytelling_shapes_our_behavior

- Pearson-Glaze, P. (Last revised 2021, February 25). *Lactation after Stillbirth and Infant Loss*. Breastfeeding Support. Retrieved 2023, from https://breastfeeding.support/lactation-after-stillbirth-infant-loss/

- Planned Parenthood of Michigan. (n.d.). *Caring for Yourself after an Abortion*. Retrieved 2023, from https://www.plannedparenthood.org/planned-parenthood-michigan/healthcare/abortion-services/caring-for-yourself-after-an-abortion

- Pregnancy Birth & Baby. (n.d.). *Your Body after Stillbirth or Neonatal Death*. Retrieved 2023, from https://www.pregnancybirthbaby.org.au/your-body-after-stillbirth-or-neonatal-death#:~:text=Dealing%20with%20a%20stillbirth%20or,milk%20production%20and%20vaginal%20bleeding

- UC Davis Health. (n.d.). *Understanding Second Trimester Miscarriage*. Retrieved 2023, from https://health.ucdavis.edu/obgyn/services/family-planning/trimester_loss.html#:~:text=After%20treatment%20of%20a%20second,after%20treatment%20is%20also%20common.

- University of Washington Medicine. (n.d.). *Miscarriage: Your Treatment Options and What to Expect*. Patient Care Services. Retrieved 2023, from https://www.uwmedicine.org/sites/stevie/files/2018-11/Miscarriage.pdf

- What to Expect. (n.d.). *Postpartum Recovery Symptoms after Pregnancy Loss*. Retrieved 2023, from https://www.whattoexpect.com/pregnancy/pregnancy-loss/postpartum-recovery-symptoms-after-miscarriage/

- What to Expect. (n.d.). *Your First Period after a Pregnancy Loss*. Retrieved 2023, from https://www.whattoexpect.com/pregnancy/pregnancy-loss/first-period-after-miscarriage/

- Yale Medicine. (n.d.). *Gestational Surrogacy*. Retrieved 2023, from https://www.yalemedicine.org/conditions/gestational-surrogacy

Chapter Four:

- Black, B.P. & Wright, P., (2012). *Posttraumatic Growth and Transformation as Outcomes of Perinatal Loss*. Illness, Crisis & Loss, Vol. 20(3) 225–237.

- Bullock, B.G. (2017). *How to Stop Your Stories from Running Your Life*. Mindful. Retrieved 2023, from https://www.mindful.org/stop-stories-running-life/

- Cacciatore, et al. (2018). *From "Silent Birth" to Voices Heard: Volunteering, Meaning, and Posttraumatic Growth after Stillbirth*. Illness, Crisis & Loss, Vol. 26(1) 23–39.

- Cherry, K. (2020, July 3). *20 Common Defense Mechanisms and How They Work*. Verywell Mind. Retrieved 2023, from https://www.verywellmind.com/defense-mechanisms-2795960

- Collins Dictionary. (n.d.). *Definition of "Come to Terms With."* Retrieved 2023, from https://www.collinsdictionary.com/us/dictionary/english/come-to-terms-with

- Di Giuseppe, M. & Perry, J.C. (2021). *The Hierarchy of Defense Mechanisms: Assessing Defensive Functioning with the Defense Mechanisms Rating Scales Q-Sort*. Front. Psychol. 12:718440. doi: 10.3389/fpsyg.2021.718440. Retrieved 2023, from https://www.frontiersin.org/articles/10.3389/fpsyg.2021.718440/full

- Hospice of the Red River Valley. (n.d.). *Common Grief Reactions*. Retrieved 2023, from https://www.hrrv.org/grief-support/common-grief-reactions/

- Kavanaugh, K. & Hershberger, P., (2005). *Perinatal Loss in Low Income African American Parents*. Journal of Obstetric, Gynecologic, & Neonatal Nursing.

- Mayo Clinic. (n.d.). *Adjustment Disorders – Symptoms and Causes*. Retrieved 2023, from https://www.mayoclinic.org/diseases-conditions/adjustment-disorders/symptoms-causes/syc-20355224

- Rutten, et al. (2013) *Resilience in Mental Health: Linking Psychological and Neurobiological Perspectives.* Acta Psychiatrica Scandinavica.

- Van, P. and Meleis, A.I. (2002). *Coping with Grief after Involuntary Pregnancy Loss: Perspectives of African American Women.* Journal of Obstetric, Gynecologic, & Neonatal Nursing.

- What's Your Grief. (n.d.). *Death, Grief, and Shattered Assumptions.* Retrieved 2023, from https://whatsyourgrief.com/shattered-assumptions/

- wikiHow. (n.d.). *How to Adjust when Things Don't Go to Plan.* Retrieved 2023, from https://www.wikihow.com/Adjust-when-Things-Don%27t-Go-to-Plan

Chapter Five:

- Allahdadian, M. and Irajpour, A. (2015) *The Role Of Religious Beliefs in Pregnancy Loss.* J Educ Health Promot. 2015 Dec 30;4:99. doi: 10.4103/2277-9531.171813. PMID: 27462641; PMCID: PMC4946273.

- Baker A.W., Keshaviah A., Horenstein A., Goetter E.M., Mauro C., Reynolds C. 3rd, Zisook S., Shear M.K., Simon N.M. *The Role of Avoidance in Complicated Grief: A Detailed Examination of the Grief-Related Avoidance Questionnaire (GRAQ) In a Large Sample of Individuals with Complicated Grief.* J Loss Trauma. 2016;21(6):533–547. doi: 10.1080/15325024.2016.1157412. Epub 2016, Feb 24. PMID: 28649184; PMCID: PMC5482544.

- Bardos, et al. (2015). *A National Survey on Public Perceptions of Miscarriage.* Obstetrics & Gynecology.

- Brier, N. (1999). *Understanding and Managing the Emotional Reactions to a Miscarriage.* Obstetrics & Gynecology.

- Exploring Your Mind. (n.d.). *Strategies for Coping with Grief and Their Consequences.* Retrieved 2023, from https://exploringyourmind.com/strategies-for-coping-with-grief-and-their-consequences/

- Gipson, J.D., Koenig, M.A., Hindin, M.J. *The Effects of Unintended Pregnancy on Infant, Child, and Parental Health: A Review of The Literature.* Stud Fam Plann. 2008 Mar; 39(1):18–38. doi: 10.1111/j.1728-4465.2008.00148.x. PMID: 18540521.

- Harris, J. (2015). *A Unique Grief.* International Journal of Childbirth Education.

- Kristenson, S. (2022, October 27). *71 Coping Skills: A List for Adults to Deal with Anxiety & Stress.* Happier Human. Retrieved 2023, from https://www.happierhuman.com/coping-skills/

- Lacombe-Duncan, A., Andalibi, N., Roosevelt, L., and Weinstein-Levey, E. (2022). *Minority Stress Theory Applied to Conception, Pregnancy, and Pregnancy Loss: A Qualitative Study Examining LGBTQ+ People's Experiences.* PLOS ONE, 17(7), e0271945. Retrieved 2023, from https://doi.org/10.1371/journal.pone.0271945

- Lally, J.R., and Valentine-French, S.H. (n.d.). *Grief, Bereavement, and Mourning.* LibreTexts. Retrieved 2023, from https://socialsci.libretexts.org/Bookshelves/Psychology/Developmental_Psychology/Lifespan_Development_-_A_Psychological_Perspective_(Lally_and_Valentine-French)/10%3A_Death_and_Dying/10.10%3A_Grief_Bereavement_and_Mourning

- Lang, et al. (2001). *Weathering the Storm of Perinatal Bereavement Via Hardiness.* Death Studies, 25:6, 497–512, doi: 10.1080/07481180126859

BIBLIOGRAPHY

- Lok I.H. and Neugebauer R. *Psychological Morbidity Following Miscarriage.* Best Pract Res Clin Obstet Gynaecol. 2007 Apr;21(2):229–47. doi: 10.1016/j.bpobgyn.2006.11.007. Epub 2007 Feb 20. PMID: 17317322.

- Luchterhand, C. (2014, updated 2019). *Grief Reactions, Duration, and Tasks of Mourning.* Department of Veterans Affairs. Retrieved 2023, from https://www.va.gov/WHOLEHEALTHLIBRARY/tools/grief-reactions-duration-and-tasks-of-mourning.asp

- Mayo Clinic. (n.d.). *Clinical Depression: What Does That Mean?* Retrieved 2023, from https://www.mayoclinic.org/diseases-conditions/depression/expert-answers/clinical-depression/faq-20057770#:~:text=Depression%20ranges%20in%20seriousness%20from,depression%20or%20major%20depressive%20disorder

- Mayo Clinic. (n.d.). *Complicated Grief.* Retrieved 2023, from https://www.mayoclinic.org/diseases-conditions/complicated-grief/symptoms-causes/syc-20360374

- Mayo Clinic. (n.d.). *Depression (Major Depressive Disorder).* Retrieved 2023, from https://www.mayoclinic.org/diseases-conditions/depression/symptoms-causes/syc-20356007

- McLeod, S. (Updated, 2023, February 24). *Stress Management Techniques.* Simply Psychology. Retrieved 2023, from https://www.simplypsychology.org/stress-management.html#:~:text=Problem%2Dfocused%20coping%20targets%20the,Problem%2Dsolving

- Michigan Department of Health and Human Services. (n.d.). *Dilation and Evacuation (D&E).* Retrieved 2023, from https://www.michigan.gov/mdhhs/adult-child-serv/informedconsent/

- michigans-informed-consent-for-abortion-law/procedures/dilation-and-evacuation-de

- Molina, K. M. and Kiely, M. (2011). *Understanding Depressive Symptoms among High-Risk, Pregnant, African-American Women.* Women's Health Issues 21–4 (2011) 293–303.

- Morin, A. (Updated on 2023, February 16). *Healthy Coping Skills for Uncomfortable Emotions.* Verywell Mind. Retrieved 2023, rom https://www.verywellmind.com/forty-healthy-coping-skills-4586742

- Mughal S, Azhar Y, Mahon MM, et al. *Grief Reaction.* [Updated 2022 May 22]. In: StatPearls [Internet]. Treasure Island (FL): StatPearls Publishing; 2023 Jan. Available from: https://www.ncbi.nlm.nih.gov/books/NBK507832/

- National Cancer Institute. (n.d.). *Coping Skills.* NCI Dictionary of Cancer Terms. Retrieved 2023, from https://www.cancer.gov/publications/dictionaries/cancer-terms/def/coping-skills

- PsychCentral. (n.d.). *6 Ways to Manage Your Emotions and Improve Your Mood.* Retrieved 2023, from https://psychcentral.com/health/ways-to-manage-your-emotions#mindfulness

- PsychCentral. (n.d.). *What's the Difference between Grief and Depression.* Retrieved 2023, from https://psychcentral.com/health/grief-and-depression

- Raypole, C. (n.d.). *7 Emotion-Focused Coping Techniques for Tough Times.* Retrieved 2023, from https://www.healthline.com/health/emotion-focused-coping

- Robbins, T. (n.d.). *How Can I Better Control My Emotions?* Retrieved 2023, from https://www.tonyrobbins.com/ask-tony/cycle-of-meaning/

BIBLIOGRAPHY

- Science Direct. (n.d.). *Modelling the Relationship between Healthy and Unhealthy Coping Strategies to Understand Overwhelming Distress: A Bayesian Network Approach.* Journal of Affective Disorders Reports. Retrieved 2023, from https://www.sciencedirect.com/science/article/pii/S2666915320300548#:~:text=Healthy%20coping%20categories%20are%20self,%2C%20social%20withdrawal%2C%20and%20suicidality

- ScienceDirect. (n.d.). *Coping Strategies.* Retrieved 2023, from https://www.sciencedirect.com/topics/psychology/coping-strategies#:~:text=There%20are%20many%20different%20conceptualizations,religious%20coping%2C%20and%20meaning%20making

- Shear, M.K., Ghesquiere, A., and Glickman, K. (2013). *Bereavement and Complicated Grief.* Current Psychiatry Reports, 15(11), 1–7.

- Stroebe, M., and Schut, H. (1999). *The Dual Process Model of Coping with Bereavement: Rationale and Description.* Death Studies. 23(3), 197–224.

- Stroebe, M., and Schut, H. (2010). *The Dual Process Model of Coping with Bereavement: A Decade On*.* Omega Vol. 61(4) 273–289, 2010.

- Study.com. (n.d.). *Problem-Focused Coping: Examples & Strategies.* Retrieved 2023, from https://study.com/learn/lesson/problem-focused-coping-examples.html#:~:text=Problem%2Dfocused%20coping%20is%20a%20technique%20in%20which%20an%20individual,the%20morning%20before%20class%20starts.

- Sutton, J. (2020, May 29). *The Science of Coping: 10+ Strategies & Skills (Incl. Wheel).* Positive Psychology. Retrieved 2023, from https://positivepsychology.com/coping-strategies-skills/

- Therapist Aid. (n.d.). *Healthy Vs. Unhealthy Coping Strategies.* Retrieved 2023, from https://www.therapistaid.com/worksheets/healthy-unhealthy-coping-strategies

- Van, P. (2001). *Breaking the Silence Of African American Women: Healing After Pregnancy Loss.* Health Care for Women International, 22:3, 229–243, doi: 10.1080/07399330120995.

- Verywell Mind. (n.d.). *Grief Vs. Depression: Which Is It?* Retrieved 2023, from https://www.verywellmind.com/grief-and-depression-1067237

- WebMD. (n.d.). *What to Know about Disenfranchised Grief.* Retrieved 2023, from https://www.webmd.com/mental-health/what-to-know-about-disenfranchised-grief

- What's Your Grief. (n.d.). *Grief and Negative Coping.* Retrieved 2023, from https://whatsyourgrief.com/grief-and-negative-coping/

Chapter Six:

- American Psychological Association. (n.d.). *Emotional Support.* In APA Dictionary of Psychology. Retrieved 2023, from https://dictionary.apa.org/emotional-support

- Angela Hospice Home Care, Inc. (2020). *Helping Children Grieve.* Retrieved 2023, from https://angelahospice.org/wp-content/uploads/2020/05/HelpingChildrenGrieve.pdf

- Brier, N. (1999). *Understanding and Managing The Emotional Reactions to a Miscarriage.* Obstetrics & Gynecology.

- Dadnatal. (n.d.). *Miscarriages and Men: Dads Share the Emotional Effects of Miscarriage.* Retrieved 2023, from https://www.dadnatal.com/all-articles-blogs/miscarriages-and-men-dads-share-the-emotional-effects-of-miscarriage#:~:text=But%20the%20

- studies%20available%20indicate,depression%20after%20their%20partner%20miscarries.
- Fatherly. (2021, April 21). *9 Couples Therapy Exercises That Should Be in Every Couple's Repertoire*. Retrieved 2023, from https://www.fatherly.com/life/couples-therapy-exercises-try-at-home/

Chapter Seven:

- Centers for Disease Control and Prevention. (n.d.). *Positive Parenting Tips*. Retrieved 2023, from https://www.cdc.gov/ncbddd/childdevelopment/positiveparenting/index.html
- Children's Hospital of Orange County. (2021, June 10). *Talking to Children about Death: An Age-by-Age Guide*. Retrieved 2023, from https://health.choc.org/talking-to-children-about-death-an-age-by-age-guide/
- Cleveland Clinic. (2022, August 1). *How to Explain Death to a Child*. Retrieved 2023, from https://health.clevelandclinic.org/how-to-explain-death-to-a-child/
- Mayo Clinic Press. (2022, October 4). *After Miscarriage: How to Tell Your Child about Pregnancy Loss*. Retrieved 2023, from https://mcpress.mayoclinic.org/parenting/after-miscarriage-how-to-tell-your-child-about-pregnancy-loss/
- Olin, T. and Wilcox-Herzog, A. (2020, October). *Discussing Death with Young Children*. Zero to Three. Retrieved 2023, from https://www.zerotothree.org/resource/discussing-death-with-young-children/
- U.S. Department of Labor. (n.d.). *Family and Medical Leave (FMLA)*. Retrieved 2023, from https://www.dol.gov/general/topic/benefits-leave/fmla

Chapter Eight:

- American Psychological Association. (2017). *How to Find a Good Therapist.* Retrieved 2023, from https://www.apa.org/ptsd-guideline/patients-and-families/finding-good-therapist

- Black Female Therapists. (n.d.). *How to Get More Emotional Support When It Feels Like No One Is There for You.* Retrieved 2023, from https://www.blackfemaletherapists.com/how-to-get-more-emotional-support-when-it-feels-like-no-one-is-there-for-you/

- Boyes, A. (2020). *How to Get Emotional Support When You Feel You Have None.* Psychology Today. Retrieved 2023, from https://www.psychologytoday.com/us/blog/in-practice/202001/how-get-emotional-support-when-you-feel-you-have-none

- Psychology Today. (n.d.). *How to Find a Therapist.* Retrieved 2023, from https://www.psychologytoday.com/us/basics/therapy/how-to-find-a-therapist

- Scott, E. (Updated January 9, 2021). *How to Create Social Support in Your Life.* Verywell Mind. Retrieved 2023, from https://www.verywellmind.com/how-to-create-social-support-in-your-life-3144955

- Stanborough, R.J., (2020). *How to Find a Therapist: 8 Tips for the Right Fit.* Healthline. Retrieved 2023, from https://www.healthline.com/health/how-to-find-a-therapist

- Thomas, S. and González-Prendes, A.A. (2009) Powerlessness, Anger, and Stress in African American Women: Implications for Physical and Emotional Health. *Health Care for Women International, 30:1–2,* 93-113, doi: 10.1080/07399330802523709.

BIBLIOGRAPHY

- University of Washington. (Last updated, May, 2022). *How Can I Develop a Support Network?* Retrieved 2023, from https://www.washington.edu/doit/how-can-i-develop-support-network

Chapter Nine:

- American Psychological Association. (n.d.). *Grief.* APA Dictionary of Psychology. Retrieved 2023, from https://dictionary.apa.org/grief

- American Psychological Association. (n.d.). *Grief.* Retrieved 2023, from https://www.apa.org/topics/grief#:~:text=Grief%20often%20includes%20physiological%20distress,%2Dneglect%2C%20and%20suicidal%20thoughts

- American Psychological Association. (n.d.). *Mental Health.* Retrieved 2023, from https://www.apa.org/topics/mental-health

- Centers for Disease Control and Prevention. (n.d.). *About Mental Health.* Retrieved 2023, from https://www.cdc.gov/mentalhealth/learn/index.htm

- Davis, T. (2021, January 4). *9 Ways to Cultivate Emotional Wellness.* Psychology Today. Retrieved 2023, from https://www.psychologytoday.com/us/blog/click-here-happiness/202101/9-ways-cultivate-emotional-wellness

- Enlightio. (n.d.). *51 Questions to Ask about Feelings.* Retrieved 2023, from https://enlightio.com/questions-to-ask-about-feelings

- GoodTherapy. (Last updated 2018, May 2). *Trigger.* Retrieved 2023, from https://www.goodtherapy.org/blog/psychpedia/trigger

- Harvard Health Publishing. (2012). *A Guide to Getting through Grief.* Retrieved 2023, from https://www.health.harvard.edu/blog/gut-feelings-how-food-affects-your-mood-2018120715548

- Harvard Health Publishing. (2022, May 1). *What's the Connection between the Gut and Brain Health?* Retrieved 2023, from https://www.health.harvard.edu/staying-healthy/whats-the-connection-between-the-gut-and-brain-health

- Harvard Health Publishing. (2023, July 18). *The Gut-Brain Connection.* Retrieved 2023, from https://www.health.harvard.edu/diseases-and-conditions/the-gut-brain-connection#:~:text=Anger%2C%20anxiety%2C%20sadness%2C%20elation,This%20connection%20goes%20both%20ways.

- Healthline. (n.d.). *The Benefits of Holy Basil.* Retrieved 2023, from https://www.healthline.com/health/food-nutrition/basil-benefits

- Hughes, V. (2011, June 1). *Shades of Grief: When Does Mourning Become a Mental Illness*? Scientific American. Retrieved 2023, from https://www.scientificamerican.com/article/shades-of-grief/

- Madison A, Kiecolt-Glaser JK. *Stress, Depression, Diet, and the Gut Microbiota: Human-Bacteria Interactions at the Core of Psychoneuroimmunology and Nutrition.* Curr Opin Behav Sci. 2019 Aug; 28:105-110. doi: 10.1016/j.cobeha.2019.01.011. Epub 2019 Mar 25. PMID: 32395568; PMCID: PMC7213601.

- Mayo Clinic. (n.d.). *Adjustment Disorders.* Retrieved 2023, from https://www.mayoclinic.org/diseases-conditions/adjustment-disorders/symptoms-causes/syc-20355224#:~:text=Adjustment%20disorders%20are%20stress%2Drelated,at%20work%20or%20at%20school.

- McLean Hospital. (n.d.). *Yes, There Is a Big Difference between Mental Health and Mental Illness.* Retrieved 2023, from https://www.mcleanhospital.org/essential/mental-health-mental-illness

- Medical News Today. (n.d.). *What Is Mental Health?* Retrieved 2023, from https://www.medicalnewstoday.com/articles/154543

- Naidoo, U. (2019, March 27). *Gut Feelings: How Food Affects Your Mood*. Retrieved 2023, from https://www.health.harvard.edu/blog/gut-feelings-how-food-affects-your-mood-2018120715548

- National Institute of Mental Health. (n.d.). *Caring for Your Mental Health*. Retrieved 2023, from https://www.nimh.nih.gov/health/topics/caring-for-your-mental-health#:~:text=Self%2Dcare%20means%20taking%20the,illness%2C%20and%20increase%20your%20energy

- National Library of Medicine. (n.d.). *Adjustment Disorder*. Retrieved 2023, from https://medlineplus.gov/ency/article/000932.htm#:~:text=Adjustment%20disorder%20is%20a%20group,type%20of%20event%20that%20occurred

- National Sleep Foundation. (Updated 2023, August 8). *Mental Health and Sleep*. Retrieved 2023, from https://www.sleepfoundation.org/mental-health

- Psych Central. (n.d.). *12 Journal Prompts for Emotional Health and Wellness*. Retrieved 2023, from https://psychcentral.com/blog/journal-prompts-to-heal-emotions

- Taylor Counseling Group. (2021, June 18). *Mental Health Vs. Mental Illness: The Difference and Why It Matters*. Retrieved 2023, from https://taylorcounselinggroup.com/blog/mental-health-vs-mental-illness/

- WebMD. (2021, June 29). *How Grief Can Affect Your Health*. Retrieved 2023, from https://www.webmd.com/mental-health/ss/slideshow-grief-health-effects

- World Health Organization. (2022, June 17). *Mental Health*. Retrieved 2023, from https://www.who.int/news-room/fact-sheets/detail/mental-health-strengthening-our-response

Chapter Ten:

- Britannica. (n.d.). *Religion*. Retrieved 2023, from https://www.britannica.com/topic/religion

- Dictionary.com. (n.d.). *Religion*. Retrieved 2023, from https://www.dictionary.com/browse/religion

- Ghaderi A., Tabatabaei S.M., Nedjat S., Javadi M., Larijani B. *Explanatory Definition of the Concept of Spiritual Health: A Qualitative Study In Iran*. J Med Ethics Hist Med. 2018 Apr 9; 11:3. PMID: 30258553; PMCID: PMC6150917.

- Healthline. (n.d.). *The Benefits of Guided Imagery and How to Do It*. Retrieved 2023, from https://www.healthline.com/health/guided-imagery

- History.com Editors. (2017, October 12). *Buddhism*. Retrieved 2023, from https://www.history.com/topics/religion/buddhism

- History.com Editors. (2017, October 13). *History of Christianity*. Retrieved 2023, from https://www.history.com/topics/religion/history-of-christianity

- History.com Editors. (2017, October 6). *Hinduism*. Retrieved 2023, from https://www.history.com/topics/religion/hinduism

- History.com Editors. (2018, January 5). *Islam*. Retrieved 2023, from https://www.history.com/topics/religion/islam

- History.com Editors. (2018, January 5). *Judaism*. Retrieved 2023, from https://www.history.com/topics/religion/judaism

- Jai Medical Systems. (n.d.). *Health Benefits of Reducing Your Screen Time*. Retrieved 2023, from https://jaimedicalsystems.com/health-benefits-of-reducing-your-screen-time/#:~:text=Better%20Focus%20and%20Brain%20Function&text=In%20turn%2C%20you%20may%20feel,focus%20on%20tasks%20without%20distraction

- Johns Hopkins Medicine. (n.d.). *Imagery*. Retrieved 2023, from https://www.hopkinsmedicine.org/health/wellness-and-prevention/imagery#:~:text=Guided%20imagery%20is%20most%20often,from%20a%20qualified%20imagery%20practitioner

- Madhav KC, Sherchand SP, Sherchan S. *Association between Screen Time and Depression among US Adults*. Prev Med Rep. 2017 Aug 16;8: 67–71. doi: 10.1016/j.pmedr.2017.08.005. PMID: 28879072; PMCID: PMC5574844.

- Mayo Clinic Health System. (2021, May 21). *5 Ways Slimming Screen Time Is Good for Your Health*. Retrieved 2023, from https://www.mayoclinichealthsystem.org/hometown-health/featured-topic/5-ways-slimming-screen-time-is-good-for-your-health

- Medical News Today. (n.d.) *5 Relaxation Techniques to Try*. Retrieved 2023, from https://www.medicalnewstoday.com/articles/5-relaxation-techniques-to-try#benefits-of-relaxation-techniques

- Mindful.org. (n.d.). *How to Meditate*. Retrieved 2023, from https://www.mindful.org/how-to-meditate/

- National Geographic Society. (n.d.). *Buddhism*. Retrieved 2023, from https://education.nationalgeographic.org/resource/buddhism/

- Stibich, M. (Updated November, 2022). *What Is Religion? The Psychology of Why People Believe.* Verywell Mind. Retrieved 2023, from https://www.verywellmind.com/religion-improves-health-2224007

Chapter Eleven:

- Price-Mitchell, M., (2018, March). *Goal-Setting Is Linked to Higher Achievement.* Psychology Today. Retrieved 2023, from https://www.psychologytoday.com/us/blog/the-moment-youth/201803/goal-setting-is-linked-higher-achievement
- Riopel, L. (2019, June). *The Importance, Benefits and Value of Goal Setting.* PositivePsychology.com. Retrieved 2023, from https://positivepsychology.com/benefits-goal-setting/
- The Peak Performance Center. (n.d.). *Benefits of Goal Setting.* Retrieved 2023, from https://thepeakperformancecenter.com/development-series/skill-builder/personal-effectiveness/goal-setting/benefits-of-goal-setting/

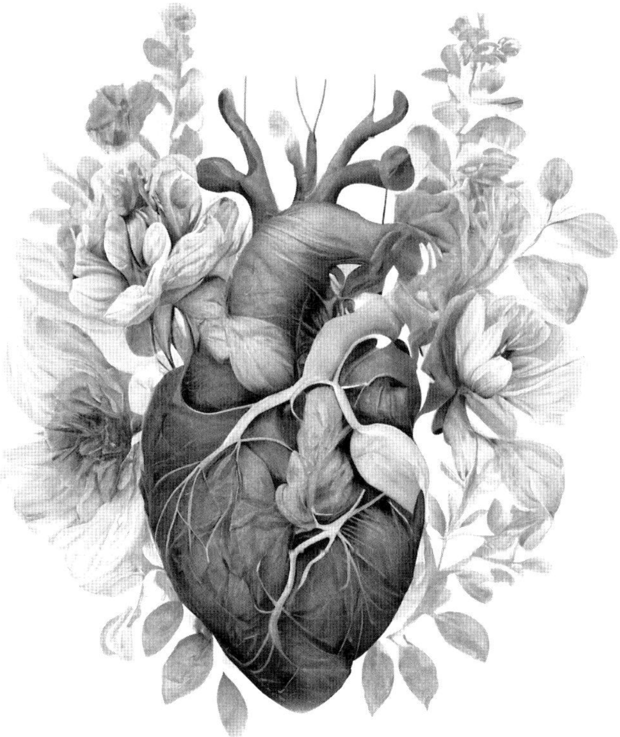